BORN TO
PREACH

BORN TO
PREACH

ESSAYS IN HONOR OF
THE MINISTRY OF

HENRY & ELLA
MITCHELL

EDITED BY SAMUEL K. ROBERTS

JUDSON PRESS
VALLEY FORGE, PA.

Born to Preach: Essays in Honor of the Ministry of Henry and Ella Mitchell
© 2000 by Judson Press, Valley Forge, PA 19482-0851
All rights reserved.

Bible quotations in this volume are from *The Holy Bible,* King James Version (KJV); the
New Revised Standard Version of the Bible, copyright © 1989 by the Division of Chris-
tian Education of the National Council of the Churches of Christ in the United States of
America. Used by permission. All rights reserved (NRSV); the Revised Standard Version
of the Bible, copyright © 1946, 1952, 1971, by the Division of Christian Education of the
National Council of the Churches of Christ in the U.S.A. Used by permission (RSV).

Library of Congress Cataloging-in-Publication Data

Born to preach : essays in honor of the ministry of Henry and Ella Mitchell / edited by
Samuel K. Roberts.
     p. cm.
    Includes bibliographical references.
    ISBN 0-8170-1368-7 (pbk. : alk. paper)
    1. Afro-American preaching. I. Roberts, Samuel K. II. Mitchell, Henry H. III.
Mitchell, Ella.

BV4208.U6 .B67 2000
251'.0089'96073 – dc21

                                                     00-055469

Printed in Canada
06   05   04   03   02   01   00
10 9 8 7 6 5 4 3 2 1

CONTENTS

INTRODUCTION

Among the immense rewards for laboring in the groves of academe are the esteem and admiration of friends and colleagues. With such esteem comes a respect for one's mind, heart, and the passion with which one attends to the demands of vocation. Among the friends of Ella and Henry Mitchell are to be counted the members of the faculty of the Samuel DeWitt Proctor School of Theology of Virginia Union University. It was at Virginia Union that Henry served as dean of the School of Theology from 1982 to 1986 and as professor of history and homiletics and Ella as associate professor of Christian education and director of continuing education during those same years.

When the faculty decided in the fall of 1998 to honor Henry and Ella Mitchell at the John Malcus Ellison Convocation in Preaching in the year 2000, it was agreed that the best way to honor them would be for faculty members to write essays from the perspective of their respective disciplines that explored the wondrous task of preaching. Consequently, the reader will find in these essays virtually all of the aspects of the perspectives on preaching inherent in theological education. Moreover, since the essays that appear in this volume come from the vocational fiber of men and women whose lives have been shaped deeply by the African American religious experience, this volume represents a unique contribution to theological education. This is so because in all probability it is the first volume of its kind produced by an African American faculty that takes seriously the import of the theological disciplines on preaching.

Both Henry and Ella Mitchell are preachers of great power and passion. Both were nurtured in an African American religious environment that reflected a deep and abiding respect for the Bible and biblical lore. Black preaching would be unthinkable without a pointed and definite focus on God's will as perceived in the biblical record. The rise of biblical criticism has engendered an erosion of biblical authority for many Christians. Sensing this crisis, Boykin Sanders explores the relationship between biblical criticism and preaching and ponders the question, What in the world is preaching the gospel? Both Jerome Ross and Robert Wafawanaka are sensitive to the cultural context in which the appropriation of biblical testimony takes place. Ross reminds us of the startling similarities between the social and cultural context of the ancient Yahwists and the contemporary context of African Americans. Wafawanaka, a Zimbabwean-born scholar, enlarges the context of the similarities somewhat by focusing on historic and contemporary paradigms for understanding poverty in ancient Israel and in traditional African societies. He and Ross affirm the proposition that valid preaching must be faithful to the biblical vision for justice.

Preaching is an art form that urges human beings to encounter each other and the divine in a moral universe undergirded by the transcendent. In an attempt to penetrate into the essence of this art form, Miles Jones suggests that preaching represents a powerful confluence of one person's utterance and another's reception of that utterance; as a servant, the preacher submits the statement of the sermon to another. Nathan Dell, like Jones, a seasoned and solid preacher, submits a sermon, inviting us to repair to a solitary place as an expression of our recognition that preaching arises from both our exposure to culture and our cloistered contact with the divine. Samuel Roberts suggests that inherent in the act of preaching is a goal of facilitating a moral transformation within the hearer, a transformation that cannot be accomplished unless the preacher has moral authority and merits the trust of the hearers. Victoria Pratt brings the sensibilities of an artist to her perception of the role sound, uttered and subliminal, plays in preaching, as she taps into the African consciousness that is yet vibrant in the Diaspora.

Ella Mitchell has been regarded almost universally as the dean of black women preachers. Her quiet demeanor belies a boldness when she mounts the pulpit. Ella has been hailed by countless black women preachers who have sought to find their own voice in a profession that has historically been dominated by men. Patricia

Gould-Champ, who in addition to her teaching tasks at the School of Theology has also planted a church, explores the dynamics in finding this voice. Alison Gise Johnson decries the historical and cultural forces that have made women preachers "invisible" and proposes a womanist hermeneutical project that can mitigate and reverse this historical process.

There is a reciprocal relationship between preaching and the vibrancy of life within the body of believers known as the church. Preaching enlivens the church, and the church provides the forum for enlivened preaching. Both Henry and Ella have lived out their professions within the contexts of vibrant churches. As a Christian educator, Ella is particularly sensitive to the dynamics at work when the church is nurtured by the preached word of God. Gloria Taylor explores this nexus between preaching and church life, advancing a belief that preaching must be considered within the educational function of the church.

The contributors and I wish to thank several persons without whom this volume could not have been completed. Dr. John W. Kinney, dean of faculty, pointed us to a source for financial support for this project. Our deep gratitude goes to the Reverend Charles Smith, distinguished visiting fellow at the Samuel DeWitt Proctor School of Theology from the American Bible Society, for a generous grant to support the writing and research. We wish to thank Mrs. Laura Davis and Mrs. Tyra Justice, faculty office associates, and Mr. Adam Bond, a student in the School of Theology, for clerical and technical assistance. Finally, for their enthusiasm and editorial discernment, our thanks go to Mr. Randy Frame and Ms. Rebecca Irwin Diehl of Judson Press. And, to be sure, the acknowledgments would not be complete if we did not recognize the historic contributions of Ella and Henry to theological education in general and to the task of preaching in particular. Through pen and pronouncement, they have inspired countless persons to hone their crafts in order that God would be glorified whenever a preacher dares to proclaim God's Word.

Samuel K. Roberts
Editor

CHAPTER I

BIBLICAL CRITICISM AND THE ART OF PREACHING
What in the World Is Preaching the Gospel?

BOYKIN SANDERS

W hen I was a seminary student my homiletics professor, a most provocative teacher to say the least, used to say that preaching is *the Word of God on contemporary issues*. For another scholar, Harold Freeman, the source for the proclamation of that Word of God is the Bible, which the preacher must interpret if the sermon is to be effective vis-à-vis contemporary issues. Freeman asserts: "Any sermon is a biblical sermon if it confronts the hearers with an accurate interpretation of the Biblical revelation and its present meaning."[1] For Fred B. Craddock preaching is "making present and appropriate the revelation of God" (Freeman's biblical revelation),[2] since "preaching brings the Scriptures forward as the living voice in the congregation."[3] "The living voice" is likely to become clear, according to Craddock, when and if the preacher devotes sufficient time in gathering that voice through exegesis of the Scriptures, "the Word of God."[4] Accordingly, Leonora Tubbs Tisdale states:

> Preaching, then, has to do with the construction of meaning. Its meaning is not **"invented"** or **created** *ex nihilo*. Rather, meaning in preaching is forged in a metaphysical way as two things which had not previously been placed side-by-side — namely a particular text (or texts) and a particular congregation context — are allowed to live together and talk together and dance with one another in the imagination of the preacher, until something new occurs through the encounter.[5]

Thus preaching is more likely to take place when a text is properly interpreted and appropriately transmitted to a waiting congregation. The transfer of what is birthed through exegesis is considered, in the parlance of homiletics, to be a responsible utterance of the Word of God or what Lucy Atkinson Rose calls "conversational preaching."[6]

But what is missing in such a portrait regarding preaching is that almost nothing is said about what should occupy the preacher and preaching task in the first place — the gospel. Rather the overwhelming emphasis is on whether one has adequately accounted for texts in their contexts, meanings of texts according to the rules of critical exegesis, and whether the preacher has meticulously observed audience issues in the preaching moment. This chapter attempts to reenter into the equation of homiletics its missing aspect, that is, What is the gospel? or What is preaching the gospel? as an important and integral topic for homiletic aims. As an essay in detection, it first seeks to show why the gospel or the preaching of the gospel became a nonissue in homiletic discussions (and perhaps for those who are trained in homiletics) by focusing on factors that contributed to this neglect. It then addresses its major concern by ferreting out earliest canonical responses to the question. Finally, it offers three possibilities for the preaching task based on our ferreted-out findings.

PREACHING AS ACCOUNTABILITY

In discussing the causes for the Renaissance in Europe (c. 1450–1670), Norman Davies in his voluminous work, *Europe: A History*, notes:

> They can be related to the growth of cities and of late medieval trade, to the vice of rich and powerful capitalist patrons, to technical progress which affected both economic and artistic life. But the source of spiritual developments must be sought above all in the spiritual sphere. Here, the malaise of the Church, and the despondency surrounding the Church's traditional teaching, becomes the major factor. It is no accident that the roots of the Renaissance and Reformation alike are found in the realm of ideas.[7]

Davies went on to describe the Renaissance as a period of new learning with three novel features:

> One was the cultivation of the long neglected classical authors, especially of Cicero and Homer who had not attracted the medieval schoolmen. The

second was the cultivation of ancient Greek as an essential part of Latin. The third was the rise of biblical scholarship based on a critical study of the original Hebrew and Latin texts.[8]

In fact the Renaissance and Reformation initiated the age of dismantling church traditions and beliefs that, in many instances, had been in place and unchanged since the end of the ancient world (476 C.E.). Characterized as an age of new learning and change through observation and human reasoning, it birthed skeptics, agnostics, and atheists vis-à-vis religion and church traditions simply because newly discovered facts through experience and experimenting made traditional thinking and believing untenable. English Deists, for example, because of new views about the behavior of the universe discarded the idea that God was personally involved in managing the world as the church had taught. While acceding the possibility that God created the universe, new facts forced the Deists to compare God's relationship to creation thereafter to a clockmaker's relationship to a clock: "Like a clockmaker, He has set the machine in motion, and now allows it to work on its own."[9]

Thus new learning allowed little room for an unseen and all-knowing God guiding the universe by some preordained plan. Mysterious phenomena, such as the New Testament story of Jesus walking on the water or the Old Testament story regarding the nonmovement of the sun in the story of Joshua, came under attack because such ideas did not square with the observations and discoveries of scientifically minded persons. Indeed, new learning in geology could prove that a six-day creation was questionable based on what the earth's layers exhibited. These layers showed that earth was not only much older than the Bible allowed but that the earth arrived at its present state and shape through processes spanning millions of years. Charles Darwin's investigations, especially his work on the origin of species, pointed in the same direction. For Darwin all living things assumed their present shape over a long period of time, with environment playing a major role. Befitting this spirit Lloyd M. Graham argues in the contemporary period that the Bible could hardly be the Word of God. Comparative religious method, thanks to science, shows that the bulk of "the Word of God" preexisted in other traditions, for example, the Adam and Eve story, the Flood story.[10] For that reason, Graham goes beyond traditional skeptics to say that the Bible is a hoax created by priests to keep people from knowing the truth. For Graham neither modern science nor higher learning is the tool to end the hoax:

> The only weapon that can destroy it [the Bible] is greater knowledge than that of its authors, and the only time is when the race acquires such knowledge of natural Causation and Creation as will render scriptural supernaturalism unnecessary; it must become so aware of the evolutionary genesis of moral qualities that it can no longer accept the scriptural account of their sources.[11]

But how would the church defend against charges regarding the nontenability of its traditions and beliefs vis-à-vis evidence according to science? Essentially the church in the Renaissance and Reformation period kept to its old ways of thinking and believing. However, in the nineteenth and twentieth centuries Bible scholars mounted a counteroffensive against skeptics of biblical traditions under the rubric of historical criticism. For more than a century these Bible scholars would talk about the Bible and the Bible world in terms that doubting skeptics and philosophers vis-à-vis church dogma found less offensive. The objectives of these scholars were essentially two: to offer reasoned explanations for biblical texts as they appeared in the Bible; and to defend the character of biblical traditions based on the context presuppositions of biblical traditions themselves.

Guided by those objectives critical scholars of the Bible would behave like archaeologists. They subjected the Bible and its traditions to the test requirement of concrete evidence as proof. Starting from latest or final stages of biblical traditions, these scholars by means of certain tools for biblical excavating (e.g., text, source, form, redaction, canonical, and social scientist techniques) peeled off layer after layer of biblical evidence in search for truths regarding biblical traditions. However, unlike skeptics and atheists who saw no merit in holding onto biblical beliefs and traditions that conflicted with reason and the known, critical scholars would concede the point but would go on to defend them.[12] A good illustration of this approach can be found in the introductory section of the New Revised Standard Version translation (The HarperCollins Study Bible [1993]) as the translators seek to make sense of Old Testament material:

> The most famous and controversial of the hypotheses that emerged was a reconstruction of four extended sources that, its advocates proposed, had been brought together over a period of centuries and through several distinct stages of editing and "redaction" to produce the Pentateuch (or, in other versions of the theory, the Tetrateuch, Genesis-Numbers, or the Hexateuch, Genesis-Joshua). Beginning with the observations that some passages used almost exclusively the name represented by the Hebrew letters YHWH to speak of God, while others used mostly a common Semitic word for divine being, but in the plural form, 'Elohim,' these scholars guessed that these passages had originally belonged to separate documents. These hypothetical documents, which also differed in other characteristics of both style and content, were accordingly labeled "J" for "Yahwist" (because j in German and neo-Latin is pronounced like Hebrew y) and "E" for "Elohist." A later source, called "D" by the scholars, was identified with an early version of the book of Deuteronomy. The fourth and latest document, thought to serve as the framework for the final stage of editing the whole Pentateuch, was intensely concerned with cultic matter, especially rules for priests and temple, so it was called "P" for "priestly." (Introduction, xx)

Here scholars of the type posited that the oldest tradition of the Old Testament, the "J" material, reflects sociopolitical and theological interest of the Israelite nation from the tenth century B.C.E.; and the final form, the "P" material, reflects priestly concerns from the fifth century B.C.E.[13]

Critical scholars of the New Testament followed a similar path of accountability. Using a comparative method for studying the Gospels, for example, the majority accorded to Mark the status of being the first written Gospel (c. 70 C.E.) followed by Matthew and Luke, and then John. Further back is the oral stage of the tradition and the story of what happens to material before it comes to rest in written form, such as in the Gospels. And still further back, indeed at the bottom of the pile, lies the subject of the Gospels — Jesus of Nazareth. Critics say that that one — the historical Jesus of first-century Palestine — can be distinguished from Christ of Christian faith by plying critical-historical methods. In that light the Jesus Seminar group claimed with certainty: "Jesus was a Galilean peasant who wrote nothing. His native tongue was Aramaic. Whereas the records of what he said exist only in Greek... the tradition has preserved only a few Aramaic words attributed to Jesus."[14]

Furthermore the Seminar is reasonably sure that Jesus, the Galilean peasant, preached the kingdom of God in his day. And beyond these truths is Jesus in the hands of the church. The group sums up the situation as follows:

> Jesus talked about the kingdom of God.
>
> The disciples talked about Jesus talking about the kingdom of God.
>
> Christian communities talked about the disciples talking about Jesus talking about the kingdom of God.[15]

For that reason scholars of the critical-historical school more often thought of our New Testament Gospels as ecclesiastical portraits consisting of legends and myths. In this way, biblical scholars like archaeologists would focus on unearthing evidence and explaining what was discovered. A typical procedure for sorting out and classifying the Jesus material is as follows:

> Working backwards requires that we search the written texts for clues of what transpired in their formation, of what took place during the oral period preceding and paralleling the first written gospels, and finally, of what traces may be left of Jesus' own activity in our sources. Jesus' own words lie, as it were, at the bottom of the layers of tradition.[16]

Yet a truth still stood that critical scholars found unavoidable: The Bible contains myths and legends that modernists often found incredulous. In other words, what is one to do with a Bible with a trove of material that critical thinkers find unintelligible and unacceptable? Within the framework of neo-orthodox apologetics (the Bible is the Word of God), Rudolph Bultmann would address the New Testament side of the problem in his demythologizing proposal of 1953.[17] Seeking to meet the scientifically minded on their terms, Bultmann asserted that myth did not mean untruth, as rationalists had assumed. Rather myths of the Bible were vehicles used by primitive peoples to convey truth and meaning. "The real purpose of myth," he said, "is not to present an objective picture of the world as it is, but to express man's understanding of himself in the world in which he lives."[18] Accordingly, the purpose of myth is "to speak of a transcendent power which controls the world and man, but that purpose is impeded and obscured by the terms in which it is expressed."[19] That "transcendent power" that myth conceals, according to Bultmann, is a great truth for first-century persons as well as contemporaries, that is, Jesus is the end of the human experience as lived "under the control of daemonic, satanic powers." In fact, Satan's term has come to an end "and the new [is] ushered in by the coming of the Messiah."[20] Thus, all humans, the rationalists and the nonquestioning, are invited to begin a fresh start with God.

What was left for Bultmann to explain is why the Gospels and other biblical sources chose the hard road of myth to package the great truth. For Bultmann myths, for example, the virgin birth in Matthew, are simply "an attempt to express the meaning of the historical figure of Jesus and the events of his life."[21] Beneath the surface of such a myth resided a cross-resurrection thematic, and this theme organized and gave shape to New Testament literature. Existentially expressed, the cross and resurrection of Jesus signified the end of old existence and the beginning of a new life.[22] Thus Bultmann offered critics of New Testament myths a new way of viewing what was perceived as incredible or nonrational: "We can see meaning in them only when we ask what God is trying to say to each one of us through them."[23]

Nonetheless the meticulous and methodical way scholars went about unearthing the world of the Bible and fixing meanings for texts placed general readers at a disadvantage vis-à-vis biblical interpretation. Only those approved by the guild were considered qualified to raise questions of biblical material and supply answers to those questions. For example, the works of Bultmann and Martin Dibelius virtually became law and gospel for classification and discussion of Gospel materials. Bultmann in particular was not only sure about the situation in life for each Gospel writer but spoke authoritatively about the origin of Gospel material as well as its use before it appeared in each Gospel. He could point with precision to the editor's hand in the putting together each Gospel, underline all alterations and embellishments in each Gospel, and say which pieces of the tradition belonged to Hellenistic circles of the church and which to Palestinian ones.[24]

Joachim Jeremias (like Bultmann and Dibelius) was no less sure about the parables of Jesus. Influenced by this concern for precision in his work on the parables of Jesus, Jeremias took the parable of the laborers of the vineyard in Matthew 20:1–16 and stated with authority that the focus of that parable was not "a call to the vineyard." Rather its focus is "the distribution of the wage at the end of the day (vv. 8ff.)."[25] Eliminating a number of unlikely interpretations for the parable, for example,

> those based on the questionable addition of verse 16b, "Many are called but few are chosen,"
>
> those influenced by an uncritical acceptance of the parable's context, and
>
> those influenced by faulty translations,[26]

Jeremias comes to what he believes to be the key point of the parable in the question raised by Jesus in verse 15a: "Am I not allowed to do what I choose with what belongs to me?" (NRSV). For Jeremias then the parable is about the vineyard owner's compassion for those who idle the day away:

> It is because of his pity for their poverty that the owner allows them to be paid a full day's wages. In this case the parable does not depict an arbitrary action, but the behavior of a large-hearted man who is compassionate and full of sympathy for the poor. Thus, says Jesus, is how God deals with men. This is what God is like, merciful.[27]

The insistence that biblical texts are to be heard in their context and are to be interpreted based on the best offerings of the scholarly guild would have tremendous impact on the preaching task. In fact what critical-historical scholars considered as important for the biblical field was distilled and transferred by homiletic scholars as guide for the preaching task. For example, homiletic scholars would advise that no sermon was ever to be attempted without "an accurate" interpretation of the biblical texts and a system of delivery which showed that the preacher was sensitive to rationalist concerns.

Furthermore, the preacher was urged to seek "truths" for the sermon by turning to commentaries, articles, and monographs produced by reputable biblical scholars, that is, critical-historical scholars. Otherwise the preacher would probably miss first things of God's Word unearthed by those who were qualified to lay it bare by means of "accurate exegesis." Craddock, for instance, offered a checklist of things for the preacher before any sermon is attempted. It included the selection of the text, determining the parameters of the text, understanding the text in its context (literary, historical, and theological), becoming aware of one's contact with the text, and putting the text in one's own words.[28] When these requirements are fulfilled, Craddock urged the preacher to move on to the task of structuring a sermon for the congregation based on "truths" discovered. So like critical-historical scholars of the Bible who focused on re-present biblical texts on their terms Craddock and others challenged the preacher to honor biblical intentions in the sermon. Only if one knew what the text meant in its more ancient biblical setting could one know what it means for a contemporary one. Preaching is the appropriation of "what the text meant" in contemporary terms for a particular congregation.[29]

Homiletic scholars would pattern their work along the lines of biblical scholars in yet another way. For instance, critical scholars of the Bible had long recognized forms in biblical literature and that each form spoke volumes about communities that preserved them. Homiletic teachers, concerned that preachers recognize the various genres unearthed by biblical critics, began to insist that preachers honor the relationship between text form (form criticism) and text function. So as biblical scholars talked more and more about forms, homiletic scholars talked more and more about delivery systems for those forms. In this way these scholars sought to get beyond one homiletic form, that is, the three points and a conclusion of traditional homiletics. Here it was stressed that when the preacher preached on a parable, for example, the system for the sermon was to be different from the one the preacher would use to preach on a miracle. To do otherwise would dishonor the text form. And even worse, one risked missing the "truth" of the text.[30] The preacher would fail in his or her responsibility to offer audiences in a preaching context what they already know and benefit from in other contexts.[31]

But in the end emphases of this kind caused homiletic scholars and the homiletically trained to leave untouched the task of preaching itself — the preaching of the gospel. Rather preaching would come to signify duties and strategies unrelated to the gospel, thanks to critical-historical scholarship. The first of these is that preaching became associated with unearthing the meaning of a more ancient biblical text and transporting that meaning from its more ancient setting to contemporary contexts. And the second is that preaching became preoccupied with appropriate delivery systems, especially whether one had been faithful or unfaithful to those systems. However, an exhibit of faithfulness to the ways and emphases of biblical criticism vis-à-vis biblical texts or the Bible as a requirement for the preaching moment cannot be equated with preaching the gospel. Rather it is more likely to reflect a defense in the court of skeptics and atheists.

Preaching as Accommodation

Since the 1970s a noticeable shift in emphasis began to take place in biblical criticism (and in preaching also, as I shall show below). In biblical criticism the shift entailed a move away from the questions and concerns of historical-critical method to the newer concerns of literary criticism. Rather than insisting on one meaning or "approved meanings" a biblical text(s) had to have as historical-critical scholars urged, literary critical scholars insisted on valuing interpretations of all interpreters. As prerequisite for biblical interpretations, literary-critical method did not require the interpreter to have knowledge of the author who wrote a book, the circumstances that gave rise to its content, the author's intent for the audience in the book, or knowledge about the book's first readers. Rather, literary critical scholars recognized the self-standing value of each biblical book and text apart from its alleged author as well as the role each reader/interpreter plays in according meaning to a text. Thus, whereas critical-historical scholarship urged distance between the text and the interpreter to ensure an "accurate" or a "nonprejudicial" reading of a biblical text, literary criticism recognized the provisional character of all interpretative outcomes and the role of the interpreter in each. Here there is no interpretation but interpretations based on the social, political, and cultural location of the interpreter. Edgar V. McKnight describes what distinguishes the critical-historical method from literary-critical method: "To read a text as history is to read it as a specific event, as what happened to particular individuals in geographically and temporally limited contexts. To read a text as literature is to read it as universal truth."[32]

By insisting that all persons have a right to enter the classroom of interpretation, literary critics prepared the way for newer voices of biblical interpretation, inside and outside of the academy. These late twentieth-century voices came in the form of feminist and womanist, continental and diaspora African, Latin and Native American, revolutionary and counterrevolutionary interpretative challenges to the mainstream voice of the biblical guild.[33] Yet the newer voices were aware of counterchallenges from the voice of the guild, especially its hesitancy to admit all readings as proper readings of a text so sacred as the divine Word. The guild would argue not for any reading but for a range of accepted readings.[34] The writers of the Postmodern Bible dramatize the tension:

> We wrote out of concern about systems of power — institutional, ecclesiastical, cultural — that authorize or block what can be said or written about the Bible. We wrote out of concern about the politics of inclusion and exclusion that determine whose reading of the Bible counts, whose does not and why. We wrote eager to see explicit acknowledgement of ethical stances, ideological positionings, self-critical and self-reflective consciousness, and affirmations of the positive values of difference and multiplicity. Most important, we wrote out of concern to make sense of the Bible in a cultural context for which there can be no detailed, comprehensive, or full accurate road map.[35]

The insistence of the new voice of literary criticism that there be "readings" — not one reading — and voices — not one voice — spilled over into the field of homiletics in unique ways. As with literary critics, new voices in the homiletic field became suspicious of the voice of the preacher as the voice in the preached word. The image of the preacher as a Moses who goes to the mountain to receive "the Word" from God was resisted. Equally resisted was the idea that what the preacher obtained in the mountain chat with

God should be delivered without audience input. The "thus says we" was more preferred than the "thus says the Lord to me."

But what would this new trend mean for homiletic counseling? First, the new voices in homiletics insisted that preachers show respect for their audiences by incorporating variety in delivery systems for sermons. They counseled that while the old three points and a conclusion method was valid for some sermons, it was not proper as a delivery system for all. In fact they advised that the delivery system of a sermon should correspond with the genre of the sermon text.[36] Second, these voices counseled preachers to be cognizant of and sensitive to the values of all persons within the preaching context — a point that literary critics had made about honoring and valuing interpreters and their interpretations. Here the newer voices insisted that preachers exhibit sensitivity to needs of parishioners by making sure that their sermons incorporated their values and concerns. Tisdale underscored the point as follows:

> Our quest, then, is for preaching that is more intentionally contextual in nature — that is, preaching which not only gives serious attention to the interpretation of biblical texts, but which gives equally serious attention to the interpretation of congregation and their sociocultural contexts, preaching which not only aims towards greater "faithfulness" to the gospel of Jesus Christ, but which also aims toward greater "fittingness" (in context, form and style) for a particular congregational gathering of hearers.[37]

Thus Tisdale advised a new image for the preacher. The preacher is no longer to be thought of as an aloof figure in the congregation but as a "folk dancer." As folk dancer the preacher was to be viewed as dancing "with" the congregation as partner.[38] And as lead dancer the preacher is a choreographer. The preacher is to lead the congregation in "both a revisioning of the assumed world...in light of the language and symbols of the Christian faith, and a reinterpretation of the ancient language of the Christian faith in light of the world of the congregation."[39] Mitchell added to the construction as follows: "To draw listeners aboard, sermons must generally avoid starting out to be critical of the hearers. To give the Word ecstatic reinforcement, the sermon must also end on an affirmative note. People cannot actually be glad about what does not exist, or what is wrong, or what ought to be. The surprising good news is that celebration is the best way to motivate people to do the will of God."[40]

Third, new voices in homiletics counseled congregations and interested others to be involved in the preparation and delivery of sermons. Rose, for example, discussing the preaching task in roundtable terms, envisions the preaching assignment as an unending conversation that "consists of tentative partisan interpretations, proposals that invite additional proposals, and personal wagers aware of other wagers."[41] Furthermore, Rose argued that the content of what is preached should be controlled by those who are invited to the table: "My conviction is that control over preaching's content belongs to all the various partners of the multiple conversations preaching fosters."[42]

But the question becomes: What happens to preaching when preaching is preoccupied with satisfying the views of each person at the table, as literary critical scholars might imagine in a context of voices out in front of the text when each voice is the voice? And what happens to preaching when the preaching task becomes honoring systems of delivery according to genres of text and when correct exegesis packaged in appropriate terms becomes an all-consuming focus of the preaching task? In the latter, preaching becomes imprisoned to aims and goals of critical biblical scholarship. It comes to be thought as faithful adherence to biblical exegesis and commentary on a biblical text or texts, followed by a faithful and meticulous transport of results to contemporary audiences in terms befitting their context. In the former, preaching comes to be thought of as serving literary critical aims or pandering to the sensitivities and complexities of postmodern communities wherein multicultural questions are at stake and where concern for inclusiveness often leaves untouched the hurts of history. Here preaching becomes satisfying exegetical demands and accommodating hearers, with particular care not to offend any within the parameters of a multicultural preaching context. It becomes what David Buttrick refers to as desire to satisfy "congregational preference."[43] Either way, the major focus becomes how preaching is done rather than what is preached. The what of preaching, that is, the gospel, will occupy us for the remainder of this chapter.

The Gospel for the Preaching Task

The term *gospel* is much discussed by lexicographers and other writers on biblical and theological subjects. Often used interchangeably with the term *kerygma* (simply meaning "proclamation or preaching"), in Christian circles the term *gospel* is customarily thought of as the announcement (a proclamation) of the death, burial, and resurrection of Jesus.[44] And associated with a gospel of Jesus' death and resurrection is a salvific claim, that is, Jesus' death and resurrection saves. Thus the gospel is said by some to be "the good news that God in Jesus Christ has fulfilled his promise to Israel, and that a way of salvation is opened to all."[45] Or put another way, it "is a saving work of God in his son Jesus Christ and a call to faith in him (Romans 1:16–17)."[46]

Behind such views and speculations regarding the meaning of the term *gospel* is the Greek term *euangelion,* a term which entered into Christian usage through the New Testament writer Paul. In the pre-Christian usage on which Paul depends, the term signified a change of seasons. It not only meant "the reward received by the messenger of victory" for the good news conveyed to recipients but that a new time or a new start had come into the world. For example, it was gospel (good news) that Caesar Augustus's reign inaugurated a time of peace and happiness for the Roman people.[47] In fact Caesar's reign reversed old patterns of Roman life and history. Whereas the Republican period was most volatile and unpredictable, Caesar's reign (the beginning of the imperial period) brought peace and stability to the Roman world. In such a milieu, it is not hard to see why Jesus' appearance in Caesar's reign would be thought of as good news also. Not only is Jesus thought of by his devotees as one reversing the situations of those who were held captive by evil spirits, bad political decisions, and weariness (Matthew 11:28–30). His death and resurrection was good news that the end of the old age had come and the new age had begun.[48]

It is in that sense that Paul uses the term as an organizer of his ministry and apostolic behavior.[49] In 1 Corinthians 15:3b–5 the gospel (the good news or glad tidings) is "that Christ died for our sins in accordance with the scriptures, and that he was buried, and that he was raised on the third day in accordance with the scriptures" (NRSV). And in verse 11 of that section Paul notes that his view regarding the meaning of Jesus, including the implications of his death and resurrection, was not his own private musing but was equally shared by a wider apostolic circle. For that reason, many scholars of the critical-historical method either agreed with Dodd's outline of the earliest gospel (kerygma)

> The prophecies are fulfilled, and the New Age is inaugurated
>   by the coming of Christ.
> He was born of the seed of David.
> He died according to the Scriptures, to deliver us out of
>   the present evil age.
>   He was buried.
> He rose on the third day according to the Scriptures.
> He is exalted to the right hand of God, as Son of God and
>   Lord of the quick and the dead.
> He will come again as Judge and Saviour of men.[50]

or defined it more narrowly as the death and resurrection of Jesus for human sin: "Essentially, the kergyma is a declaration that Christ is risen from the dead, and by that great act God has bought salvation."[51]

Either way, there was the tendency among historical-critical scholars to claim that Paul's gospel concept helped to shape the Gospels of the New Testament as well. In fact the Gospels were thought of as expansions of the death-buried-resurrection theology of Paul and Pauline related communities.[52] Yet a perusal of the Gospels vis-à-vis the use of the term *gospel* reveals a more complex picture. Though Luke, for example, never uses the noun *euangelion*, the writer of that Gospel does use the verb *euangelizomai* (roughly translated "to proclaim or announce good news"). In that regard, Luke reports that an angel appeared to shepherds at the time of Jesus' birth announcing "good news" of great joy: "To you is born this day in the city of David a Savior who is the Messiah, the Lord" (Luke 2:10–11, NRSV). The first Gospel writer, Mark, can refer to the anointing action of the woman at Bethany in good news terms: "Truly I tell you, wherever the *good news* [gospel] is proclaimed *(kerychthe)* in the whole world, what she has done will be told in remembrance of her" (Mark 14:9). Certainly the usage here is nearest to Paul's "death-burial-resurrection thematic" since the anointing is related to the death and burial of Jesus (v. 8) and appears in the passion context of Mark. But the writer, Mark, can use the term *gospel* (good news) in other ways too. Jesus himself refers to a "gospel of God" — "The time is fulfilled, and the kingdom of God has come near; repent, and believe in the good news" (Mark 1:14–15, NRSV). Here the term *gospel* (the good news) refers not to the death and resurrection of Jesus but to the joyous announcement that the kingdom of God has come near in time. And strikingly the Markan writer uses the term as a caption for the Gospel of Mark itself — his work is called "the good news of Jesus Christ" (Mark 1:1, NRSV).

In the Gospel of Matthew our term is used in another way. The Jesus of that Gospel and his disciples, for instance, more often speak about "the gospel (good news) of the kingdom" (Matthew 4:23; 9:35; 10:7; 24:14). And since a reading of Matthew shows that its author focuses on endurance in the face of persecution or opposition (cf. Matthew 10:22; 24:13), it is likely that the term *gospel* (especially "the gospel of the kingdom") relates in some ways to those issues. In fact Matthew 24:13–14 makes *gospel* endurance. There the good news that is to be proclaimed throughout the world is that "the one who endures to the end will be saved" (v. 13). Of John it only needs to be said that the writer of that Gospel does not use the term *euangelion* (gospel, or good news) at all. Yet the Gospel of John is good news also.

The first point then is this: While the death-burial-resurrection thematic is powerful and controlling for what Paul means by the gospel, the Pauline concept is not always what Paul's contemporaries mean by the term. The second point is this: Even Paul himself was not preemptive and uniform in his use of the term. For example, in addressing his audience in our 2 Corinthians, Paul singled out a group whom he chose to call "super-apostles" (2 Corinthians 11:5). He admits that they are as valid as he is (he is just a better apostle than they with far more experiences; cf. 11:22–29), though they preach a "different gospel" than he does (2 Corinthians 11:4c). And in 1 Corinthians, where the term *gospel* for

Paul is tantamount to the death, burial, and resurrection of Jesus (1 Corinthians 15:3b–5), in actual usage at Corinth the gospel is for Paul the "Christ crucified" word alone (1 Corinthians 1:23; 2:2). In that community, at least, the gospel was a way of life without divisiveness (1 Corinthians 1:13).

What then does this mean for a definition of the term *gospel* in biblical usage? It simply means that the meaning the term *gospel* was given depended on the context in which it was used. That there were no particular content elements that the gospel had to contain without which there would be no gospel is clear. Thus I can agree with Rose that there is no such thing as "an unchanging kerygma" grounded in what the apostles preached in the early years of the church. Rose is also on target when she says that "the kerygma might designate a temporary formulation of a slice of God's activity in the world that is critical for the contemporary church and that is grounded in revelation as an ongoing conversation with God, the Word, and biblical texts."[53] But contrary to Rose, whose views take flight from the need to question the preacher prerogative to claim that he or she alone has a word from God apart from the involvement of the congregation, I take the position that there is also permanence in the gospel. My position here is that while kerygma simply refers to preaching as proclamation without making a judgment whether that proclamation (kerygma) is preaching the gospel, preaching the gospel is judgment. Preaching the gospel means that God in one way or another weighs our habits, schemes, and ways of life by the measure of the truth uttered through the good news word and finds all of them wanting in light of the way of primordial Eden. As such the preaching of the gospel is a call to repentance, a switch from death to life in real terms. It is the invitation to accept restructured existence as the way of the Spirit and the message to end life as we know it and begin new times.

My point then is that the gospel is not only the glad tidings of done-over existence; it is also the solid position that God unchangingly expects something "other" to be in existence within the human context. Thus, as a fullness of time concept, it is an alternative plan, indeed a reversion to God's plan for life and the good earth and an end to the reign of death and destruction. As such the gospel in real life is a world free of oppression and racism. It is the permanent "other way," the way of God, in a world of evil designs and death.

What might this view of the gospel mean for the preacher and the preaching of the gospel today? Three possibilities are given here.

It means that the first duty of the preacher is to preach the gospel. This means that the preacher should not substitute preaching the gospel, the unadulterated truth of God for a congregation, for the cover of hiding behind an accurate exegesis of a biblical text and the transport of that exegesis in palpable and acceptable terms to a waiting congregation. It is one thing to be faithful to a biblical text. It is quite another to be faithful to the gospel. For example, being faithful to the exegesis of a text could offer up a serving of racism and death as it did in the period of African enslavement in America and since. But being faithful to the gospel ends death and a world of oppression and racism. On this point Paul seems to be in agreement: "for the letter kills, but the Spirit gives life" (2 Corinthians 3:6b, NRSV).

It means that the preacher, especially in communities of the suffering due to outside forces and self-inflicted ones, must preach the good news of deliverance from all impediments. The preacher must salve sufferers, to be sure. But more importantly, the preacher must prophesy. Every attempt is to be made by the preacher both in preachments and in actions to end violence against sufferers since the gospel is revolutionary liberation. The bridle of Exodus should guide the preacher's tongue, and the preacher should always remember that a permanent plank in the gospel is deliverance from slavery — political, social, religious, economic, cultural, racial. Deliverance from these is the following of Jesus all the way. This is glad tidings of great joy today.

This means that sermons in African American contexts should have appropriate endings. In other words, sermons should not end referencing the death and resurrection of Jesus without justification. Since preaching the gospel here is viewed as the word about an alternative arrangement, especially one under the tutelage of life rather than death, the tendency of some African American preachers to end sermons in the graveyard without justification could be an exercise in not preaching the gospel. Let us admit, graveyard preaching on the fact that "Jesus died and got up early on Sunday morning" may sound like the gospel, but in real terms it can retard capabilities. Here the point is that preaching the gospel is the good news of the reversal of things as they are and the bringing of God's way into existence. It is not the utterance of a predefined formula or the exposition of a biblical text or texts.

Thus, preaching as faithfulness to text(s), as deference to systems of delivery, and as sensitivity to audience interest may indeed be preaching but not preaching the gospel. Preaching is good news.

NOTES

1. Harold Freedman, *Variety in Biblical Preaching: Innovative Techniques and Fresh Forms* (Waco, Tex.: Word, 1987), 26.

2. Fred B. Craddock, *Preaching: An Overview* (Nashville: Abingdon, 1985), 51.

3. Ibid., 27.

4. Ibid., 127–28; also Henry H. Mitchell, *Black Preaching* (New York: Harper & Row, 1979, 1970), 112, who notes: "Any understanding of Black preaching requires an adequate understanding of the Black-culture view of the Bible, because Black preaching has been centered throughout its history in the Bible. Black congregations do not ask what a preacher thinks or what is his opinion. They want to know what God has told him through his encounter with the *Word of God*" (emphasis added).

5. Leonora Tubbs Tisdale, *Preaching as Local Theology and Folk Art* (Minneapolis: Fortress, 1997), 126, emphasis added.

6. See Lucy Atkinson Rose, *Sharing the Word: Preaching in the Roundtable Church* (Louisville, Ky.: Westminster/John Knox, 1997), who postulates that the task of responsible preaching ("conversational preaching" as she calls it) is "to gather worshipers regularly around the Word, to set texts and interpretations loose in the midst of the community, so that the essential conversations of God's people are nurtured" (98). The Word here for Rose, as for most, is the Bible.

7. Norman Davies, *Europe: A History* (New York: Oxford University Press, 1996), 477.

8. Ibid., 477.

9. See A. N. Wilson, *God's Funeral* (New York and London: Norton, 1999), 122.

10. Lloyd M. Graham, *Deceptions and Myths of the Bible* (Secaucus, N.J.: Carol Publications, 1997), 5.

11. Ibid., 6.

12. For a sample of this method in Old Testament studies, see Bernard W.

Anderson (assisted by Katheryn Pfisterer Darr), *Understanding the Old Testament*, abridged 4th ed. (Upper Saddle River, N.J.: Prentice-Hall, 1998); for the New Testament, Howard Clark Kee, *Understanding the New Testament*, 5th ed. (Englewood Cliffs, N.J.: Prentice-Hall, 1993).

13. Anderson, 1–48.

14. Robert W. Funk, Bernard Brandon Scott, and James R. Butts, *The Parables of Jesus* — The Red Letter Edition — The Jesus Seminar (Sonoma, Calif.: Polebridge, 1988), 2.

15. Ibid., 4–5.

16. Ibid., 6.

17. See Rudolph Bultmann and five critics, *Kerygma and Myth: A Theological Debate*, ed. Hans Werner Bartsch (1953; New York: Harper & Row, 1961).

18. Ibid., 10.

19. Ibid., 11.

20. Ibid., 15–16.

21. Ibid., 35.

22. Ibid., 34–44.

23. Ibid., 35.

24. Rudolph Bultmann, *The History of the Synoptic Tradition*, trans. John Marsh (1931; rev. ed.; New York and Evanston: Harper & Row, 1963).

25. Joachim Jeremias, *The Parables of Jesus*, 2d ed. (New York: Charles Scribner's Sons, 1972), 34.

26. Ibid., 34–36.

27. Ibid., 37.

28. Craddock, 99–124.

29. Thus Craddock, 16, 27–29, 100; see also Mitchell, 39; and Samuel D. Proctor, *The Certain Sound of the Trumpet: Crafting a Sermon of Authority* (Valley Forge, Pa.: Judson, 1994), 19.

30. See Craddock, 170–209; and Mitchell, 37–47.

31. See Freedman, 117–24, who makes this point in noting that most parishioners can no longer deal with abstractions as they are used to a steady diet of visual imaging provided by telecommunications and the entertainment world.

32. Edgar V. McKnight, *The Bible and the Reader: An Introduction to Literary Criticism* (Philadelphia: Fortress, 1985), 10.

33. See *The New Interpreter's Bible* (Nashville: Abingdon Press, 1994), 1:125–87 for a summary of these developments. Also Brian K. Blount, *Cultural Criticism: Reorienting New Testament Criticism* (Minneapolis: Fortress, 1995), who offers good cultural and social reasons for incorporating new voices in the biblical conversation.

34. For an enlightening discussion on the issue, see *The Postmodern Bible: The Bible and Culture Collective* (New Haven, Conn.: Yale University Press, 1995), 45–51.

35. Ibid., 15.

36. For extended discussions, see Mitchell, especially 37–47 and 79–146; David Buttrick, *A Captive Voice: The Liberation of Preaching* (Louisville, Ky.: Westminster/John Knox, 1994), 76–99; Craddock, 170–93; and David J. Lose,

"Narrative and Proclamation in Post-Liberal Homiletics," *Homiletics* 22, no. 1 (1998): 1–14.

37. Tisdale, 32–33.

38. Ibid., 56–90, 124–26.

39. Ibid., 126.

40. Mitchell, 63; cf. Tisdale, 42.

41. Rose, 105.

42. Ibid., 106.

43. Buttrick, 46–49.

44. See *Baker Encyclopedia of the Bible*, Walter A. Blackwell, ed.(Grand Rapids, Mich.: Baker House Books, 1988), 2:1261.

45. See *The New Bible Dictionary*, J. D. Douglas, ed. (London: The Intervarsity Fellowship, 1962), 484.

46. See *Nelson's Illustrated Dictionary of the Bible*, Herbert Lockyer Sr., ed. (Nashville: Thomas Nelson Publishers, 1986), 438.

47. See *The New International Dictionary of New Testament Theology*, Colin Brown, ed. (Exeter, Devon, U.K.: The Paternoster Press, 1971), 2:107–8, for an insightful discussion on how social and political issues gave shape to the term in first- and second-century Christian usage.

48. See *Dictionary of Jesus and the Gospels*, Joel B. Green and Scot McKnight, eds. (Downers Grove, Ill.: InterVarsity Press, 1992), 282–86.

49. Researchers show that Paul uses the term *gospel* more than did any other New Testament writer. See the statistics in *The New International Dictionary of New Testament Theology (NIDNTT)*, 2:110, wherein it is stated that Paul used the term *euangelion* twenty-three times without qualifications. For the editor, Colin Brown, this simply means that Paul's audiences knew what Paul intended by the term. In a word, *NIDNTT* posits: "It means good news: that God has acted for the salvation (redemption) of the world in the incarnation, death and resurrection of Jesus" (111).

50. C. H. Dodd, *The Apostolic Preaching and Its Developments* (1936; Grand Rapids, Mich.: Baker, 1980), 17.

51. *Baker Encyclopedia of the Bible*, 2:1262.

52. Thus *The Interpreter's Dictionary of the Bible*, Keith Grimm, ed. (Nashville: Abingdon Press, 1976), Supplement, 370; and *The Anchor Bible Dictionary*, David Noel Freed, ed. (New York: Doubleday, 1992), 2:1077–79.

53. Rose, 103.

CHAPTER 2

THE CULTURAL AFFINITY
BETWEEN THE ANCIENT YAHWISTS
AND THE AFRICAN AMERICANS
A Hermeneutic for Homiletics

JEROME CLAYTON ROSS

The ancient Yahwists (i.e., Israelites and Judahites/Judeans) and the African Americans have a similar social situation: they are not fully self-determinant and therefore constitute minorities in their respective cultures. This one but multifaceted fact provides the basis for interpretation of the Bible for African Americans and must be considered by all who endeavor to appropriate the content of the Bible, for its import leads to a focus upon survival as a quest for freedom. In this chapter the contexts of the ancient Yahwists will be briefly examined in order to posit an identifying link with, and a biblically relevant hermeneutic for modern homiletics by, African Americans.

THE SOCIAL SITUATION OF THE ANCIENT YAHWISTS

Except for the reign of David-Solomon, the Yahwists were dominated by the superpower nations during the biblical period. These nations were organized as monarchies and are typically labeled suzerains, that is, the superior or dominant nations in their international treaties or relationships with Israel and/or Judah. Being the militarily and politically stronger parties in their respective treaties, these nations superimposed their cultures upon the nations or peoples whom they ruled, thereby establishing the standards of living for them. Categorically, the common features of their rules are the basic requirements that they imposed upon their vassals (i.e., the nations or the peoples that they dominated):

22

forced acceptance of their administrative arrangements; payment of tribute; forced acceptance of their religions; and unconditional loyalty, that is, no foreign alliances.[1] Violation of any of these constituted treason or insurrection and was severely punished. The nations that exercised suzerainty over Israel and/or Judah, in chronological order, were Egypt, Assyria, Babylonia, Persia, Greece, and Rome.

Under Egyptian imperial rule, the existence of Israel is first documented. From 1550 to 1150 B.C.E., Egypt controlled Palestine and sponsored Israel as a tribal ally that was developed by Egyptian and Palestinian chiefs for the purpose of overseeing tribal interests and the border zone between the Egyptians and the Hittites. This sponsorship did not definitively end until the time of David, who developed the first Yahwistic nation, following the collapse of the Egyptian New Kingdom, which was probably during the reign of Rameses VI (c. 1141–1133 B.C.E.).[2] This dominance of Israel by Egypt is reflected in the use of Egyptian names for Yahwists (e.g., Moshe), of the Egyptian administrative system by David as a model for organization of his monarchy, of the Egyptian temples by Solomon as a model,[3] and the presentation of Egypt as the archenemy of Israel that was conquered by Moses, who is representative of David in the biblical accounts.[4]

The next kingdom to dominate Israel and Judah was the Assyrians, whose presence was acutely felt during the reign of Omri in the north and Ahab in the south. Shalmaneser III (c. 858–824 B.C.E.) began military moves toward Palestine that ended with the dominance of Israel and Judah by Tiglath-Pileser III during the Syro-Ephraimite War of 733 B.C.E. and the destruction of Israel by Shalmaneser V in 721 B.C.E.[5] During this period, Assyrian culture impacted both Yahwistic kingdoms, further syncretizing the forms of Yahwism and perpetuating Aramaic as the international language.[6] Responses to these phenomena are reflected in the law collections,[7] the prophetic advice,[8] and the attempts at revolution by Hezekiah (720 and 701 B.C.E.) and Josiah (622 B.C.E.).

The Babylonians were the third kingdom to dominate, at this time Judah, since Israel had been destroyed. Babylonian control of Judah had already begun by the reign of Hezekiah,[9] particularly when he was spared by Sennacherib for participating in a revolt against Babylon (c. 701 B.C.E.), and continued until the destruction of Judah in 586 B.C.E.[10] Near the end of Judah, Babylonia and Egypt vied for control of Judah, precipitating divided allegiances within the Southern Kingdom.[11]

The restoration period began under the Persian regime that was led by Cyrus, who defeated the Babylonians (c. 539 B.C.E.). Since the Babylonian exile (c. 587–538 B.C.E.) and throughout the Roman period (with the exception of the Hasmonean period), the Yahwists lived in colonies, having no national identity. However, the birth of Judaism filled this void by creating and perpetuating a sociopolitical identity without the structure of a monarchy through reappropriation of the ancient Yahwistic traditions in shabbat observance, circumcision, and dietary laws.[12]

The fifth kingdom to dominate the Jews was the Greeks (c. 333–63 B.C.E.). The major challenge that the Hellenistic rulers posed to the Jews was their overt intent to Hellenize intolerantly, an intent that was propagated through the founding of Greek cities. Yahwistic identity was targeted in order to seek its eradication.[13] Obviously all Jews did not agree on how to handle this challenge, and their differences became evident in the Jewish sects that emerged.[14] The severe persecution that occurred within this diverse populace spawned apocalyptic literature as a countermeasure to apparently hopeless martyrdom.[15]

The sixth kingdom to dominate the Jews was the Romans. They continued the tone of administration that was prevalent with the Greeks and failed to create homogeneity within Judea. The corruption, violence, and inconsistency of their administration led to repeated revolts by the Jews,[16] who were fueled by belief in the God of Moses, who was hailed as the sociopolitical deliverer from Egypt; practice of laws and rituals that Moses purportedly commanded; study and practice of "sacred traditions" (i.e., the Torah, Nebiim, and Kethubim) within synagogues; regular prayer; individualism; predominance of apocalyptic eschatology; and varied sects, or religious groups (e.g., Pharisees, Sadducees, Essenes, Zealots, "pietistic extremists").[17] In this context fits Jesus, an itinerant preacher in Galilee, whose messianic-like activities led to him being accused by the Jewish authorities, before the Roman procurator, of being a political and social agitator. He started an egalitarian movement[18] among the masses (i.e., "the people of the land" [עַם־הָאָרֶץ]), from a Pharisaic posture, critiquing and condemning the Pharisees and the Sadducees,[19] which apparently ended in confrontation in Jerusalem around the time of Passover. It is very probable that he incited a riot in the temple at Jerusalem, bringing attention to his cause and thereby forcing the hands of the Jewish leaders and the Roman administration. For his efforts he received Roman capital punishment.

However, following his tragic death, his disciples created an apocalyptic sect within Judaism, based on the application of a Pharisaic belief, that is, the resurrection of Jesus. *Apologia* in the form of gospels, in defense of charges of treason that were leveled against their leader and them, were written to explain his messiahship. Substantively, they spiritualized the messianic traditions and subsumed the traditions of "the Son of God" ([בֶּן־אֱלֹהִים] 2 Samuel 7; Psalms 2, 110), "the servant of Yahweh" ([עֶבֶר־יהוה] Isaiah 42:1–4; 49:1–6; 50:4–11; 52:13—53:12), and "the Son of man" ([בֶּן־אָדָם] 1 Enoch) under that of "the Messiah" ([מָשִׁיחַ] Isaiah 9:2–7; 11). The "servant of Yahweh" passages, especially Isaiah 52:13—53:12, provided the rubric for integrating the other traditions under that of the Messiah. Eventually this sect severed its ties with its mother faith, becoming a separate religion by the time of the Jewish wars of 66–70 C.E.[20]

From this general sketch of the history of the ancient Yahwists, it is evident that they mainly lived as vassals or a dominated people. The conditions of their existence were determined by two factors: the suzerains and the local rulers. Under the supervision of the respective suzerains, which was sometimes stringent and other times lenient, the tribal and the monarchical leaders of the ancient Yahwists sought to develop and delineate strategies for surviving. The tangible evidence of this is the traditions of the Hebrew Bible and the Greek Testament, which document the diverse presentations of their faith. In no uncertain terms, the ancient Yahwists (Israelites and Judahites) constituted what today is called a minority and were not fully politically self-determinant (i.e., free). This point is the identifying link between the ancient Yahwists and the African Americans. Therefore, the fundamental thread for understanding them (and for that matter any people) and appropriating their traditions is survival.[21]

By survival I mean the perpetuation and preservation of a people in some place with a purpose that makes possible community identity. Survival is significantly determined by the balance a people maintains between its ideals and the sociopolitical circumstances that confront and challenge it. This fundamental task has seven requirements: administrative structure, that is, some sociopolitical arrangement that is designed for operation (cf. Nehemiah 8; 10; 11; Exodus 18:13–27; Leviticus 10:9–11; Numbers 8); economic independence, that is, generation, acquisition, and management of the community's supplies and demands (cf. Nehemiah 5; 10; 13:15–22; Leviticus 25); ideological standardization or intracommunal organization, that is, determination and establishment of the laws or rules for the given community (cf. Nehemiah 13:23–31a; Exodus 20:1–17; Deuteronomy 5:6–21; Exodus 21:23–25; Leviticus 24:10–23; Deuteronomy 19:21); common language, that is, the spoken tongue of the group (cf. Nehemiah 13:23–24; Judges 12:1–7); selective appropriation or assimilation of the dominant culture by the dominated culture, that is, balance of extracommunal influences and intracommunal accommodation (cf. Nehemiah 7:6–72; 10–12; Leviticus 18:1–5, 24–30; 20:22–26); people or population (cf. Nehemiah 7:6–72; 10–12; Genesis 12:1–4; Exodus 1:1–7; Leviticus 18:21–23; 20:3–5, 13, 15–16; Deuteronomy 25:5–10); and land or place (cf. Nehemiah 5; Genesis 12:1–4; 23; 50:22–26; Exodus 13:19; Leviticus 25; Joshua). Fulfillment of these requirements is normative for every people; these items must be addressed and supplied if a people are to exist meaningfully and/or be free. In other words, the quality of freedom that a people enjoys is proportionate to the number and the extent of the requirements for survival that it fulfills.

The fulfillment of the requirements for survival by the ancient Yahwists was complicated by several factors. Their society was heterogeneous. This mixed social situation prevented Yahwism from ever being monolithic and thereby spawned the various theologies in the Hebrew Bible and the Greek Testament, which are the expressions of the ancient Yahwists as they struggled to survive. Their theological concerns entailed religious matters that were intertwined with sociopolitical ones, which contributed to divisions among them. Ancient Yahwistic faith must be regarded as their ideologies for living that are manifested socially in customs, institutions, practices, and symbols and conceptually in statements or theories. The latter of these, the conceptual expressions of their faith, is their theologies, which constitute the belief statements or the doctrines that they fostered for meaningful and purposeful existence. These are the ideological arguments that they articulated and developed within their assorted historical contexts, which of necessity included and endorsed social (i.e., economic, political, cultural) action.[22] In other words, the faith of the Hebrew Bible and the Greek Testament comprises the sociopolitical propaganda of the ancient Yahwists.[23]

Again, the situation of ancient Israel and Judah was compounded by the fact that they were never fully free except during the time of David. They were continually dominated by the stronger nations and were forced to accommodate these cultures. This made fulfillment of the requirements for survival difficult, because their existence depended upon marginal compliance, at the least, with the policies of their overlords, in deference to their own standards. Thus the primary concern that is reflected in the Bible is the survival of a minority, that is, the quest for preservation and perpetuation of community identity or meaningful existence by a people who are not fully self-determinant. In modern terms, ancient Israel and Judah were Two-Thirds World countries or lesser nations among the superpowers of the ancient world. Their quest for survival pervades the Hebrew Bible, even the Greek Testament. Therefore this motif and the corresponding requirements are the agenda items that must be employed for examining the text and reappropriating their traditions.

The Hermeneutic for Homiletics

The previous section has definitively implied that thorough biblical-critical study is mandatory for homiletics. First, while biblical studies endeavors to understand the ancient texts, homiletics seeks to appropriate what is understood for use in some modern context. Second, while biblical studies is preoccupied with contextualization of the ancient propaganda, homiletics recontextualizes this data so that it may be applied in contemporary settings. Third, while biblical studies attempts to engage the foreign and ancient cultures of the Bible, homiletics employs the premises, presuppositions, and principles of the ancient Yahwistic culture(s) that are ascertained in addressing situations and concerns that are parallel. Thus homiletics builds upon biblical-critical study, sharing similar and related concerns. Biblical studies is at the service of homiletics, as the former provides the working data for the latter.

Furthermore, for the content of homiletics to be consistent with that of the ancient Yahwists, the enterprise must be informed by the agenda(s) of the ancient Yahwists. This agenda — these survival concerns — is complex and diverse; it derives from various social arenas and levels. In other words, domination by political overlords led to the grouping of the ancient Yahwists in assorted socio-politico-religious postures.[24] Generally the people could be identified as the orthodox or conservative Yahwists; the moderate Yahwists or assimilationists; and the liberal or left-wing Yahwists. These postures are based upon the degree of consistency with or deviation from the normative standards of Yahwism as established and fostered by the prevalent leaders. Included within these postures were corresponding political constructs (e.g., tribalism, monarchialism, colonialism) and economic status (e.g., the wealthy/intelligentsia, the poor, etc.) that constitute societal levels.[25] Furthermore, the varying forms of organization, including their respective cults, competed, often conflicting. In this respect there were popular forms of Yahwism that circulated in the areas surrounding the cities and that countered the monarchical forms that were fostered by a given administration.[26] The economic, the social, the political, and the religious posture of the ancient Yahwists were mutually influential and mutually determinative. Internal struggles between and within the tribal culture and the monarchic culture continued throughout the period of the monarchy, into the postmonarchic periods, spawning numerous ideological arguments that eventually were recorded as the Hebrew Scriptures.[27]

The representatives of the respective sectors of Yahwistic society acted as spokespersons, expounding and embodying the concerns of their constituency, and thereby they are paradigmatic for homiletics. The ones that are most relevant for homiletics are the prophets and the Levitical preachers. While the premonarchical priests mainly operated within the local or the state cults, the classical prophets emerged as sociopolitical activists, intellectuals, even revolutionaries, who operated from more conservative bases (most likely tribal), represented those who were exploited by the Yahwistic monarchies, and criticized the oppressive policies of the monarchies,[28] in the form of judgment speeches[29] or predictions of disaster.[30] Most of the classical prophets did not operate in some official capacity but assumed the mantle of ambassadorship under the auspices of an intuitive call. Though their operations included proclamation, they were not speakers as much as they were activist-advisers; Yahwistic prophetism was mainly Yahwistic tribalism's check on the Yahwistic monarchy. But Levitical preaching emerged within the postexilic period, probably within some rudimentary synagogue-like services,[31] in order to address the needs of the Jewish colonies in the absence of the typical Yahwistic political structures. The Levitical preachers operated as a popular-priestly component, providing instruction and theological reflection that were based upon authoritative texts. The sermonic form that they employed was a blend of the Deuteronomic[32] and the Priestly[33] styles, which consisted of some doctrine, which laid out the conditions upon which God is prepared to give assistance; the application, that is, the historical reference that shows God's nearness and distance; and the exhortation, that is, a call to faith with the promise of a reward.[34] Moreover, the orientation was toward addressing the prevalent sociopolitical issues and fulfilling the requisites for survival. This is a most potent clue for modern homiletics.

In light of this overview of the social situation of the ancient Yahwists and their efforts to address the diverse circumstances that they faced, biblical preaching was development and delineation of sociopolitical strategies that detailed the demands and the directions of Yahweh, based upon the premise that the ancient Yahwistic traditions were authentic and authoritative expressions of the Word of Yahweh. It was directed toward the survival of Israel and/or Judah, a minority people, and therefore was essentially and intentionally concerned with acquisition of freedom. In this enterprise the seven requirements for survival were inevitably undertaken as agenda items. This is paradigmatic for homiletics.

Therefore the hermeneutic for homiletics that I propose is contextualization or realism. By this I mean the appropriation of the Bible for the purpose of survival. This method is not new; for centuries its focus and the sensitivities by which it is employed have been slighted by unchecked prejudices. Here several things are necessary. The readers of the Bible must employ the results and the methods of biblical criticism and the sensitivities that I have just mentioned and continually seek to articulate the probable (i.e., reconstructed) contexts in which the statements of the Bible emerged, were written, and were used. The goal is to hear the text in context, that is, to understand the Bible as the oral or written conversations of the ancient Yahwists as they might have occurred in their various, original sociopolitical situations. These conversations necessarily reflect the issues and the agendas of the leaders of people (i.e., Israel and Judah) who are dominated by superpower nations. The primary objective, then, is to read the text — to hear it — from their postures, not ours. The operative premise is that the Bible is the expressions of some communication between speakers/writers and respective audiences, pertaining to issues that were relevant to their situations, in which the speakers/writers advocated solutions that were consistent with their sociopolitical perspectives/postures.[35]

Second, a sense of realism must be developed. The Bible must be read as a collection of communications between different and diverse parties; it must be contextualized. By locating the Bible, we are able to attribute it to somebodies. Generally we must determine what the genre of a given text is; ascertain when, where, and by whom that text was written; compare the information for reconstructing the event with the view(s) presented in the text; and deduce the purpose(s) behind the presentation of the text or the intention(s) of the writer(s). This can be done by asking and answering through thorough research the following questions: Who spoke the text? Who wrote it? To whom was it spoken? To whom was it written? For whom was it spoken? For whom was it written? When was it spoken? When was it written? Where was it spoken? Where was it written? What is it addressing? How is it presented? Why is it presented? Here, we cannot be naive. The ancient Yahwists had biases and flaws, just as we do, and their theologies reflect such. In appropriating principles and guidelines from the Bible, we must not uncritically, unduly, or necessarily embrace their biases.

Third, the requirements for survival, which I discussed earlier, must be used as the agenda items for reading the text. Know that the quality of one's freedom is determined by the extent to which one fulfills the requirements for survival. Because the ancient Yahwists spent practically their whole history as a vassal nation or people, their freedom was significantly diminished, their possessions were disproportionately distributed, and their privileges were inequitously enjoyed, as their leaders differed regarding the best courses of action in the respective situations. As homileticians, we must examine our cultural particulars, that is, our sociopolitical affiliations, our assumptions and biases, our economic status, and compare our situations with that of those in, around, and behind the text, in order to see if there is, and wherein there is, cultural compatibility and circumstantial identification between the ancient Yahwists and us.[36] Then we may critique ourselves in light of the principles that we appropriate from the Bible. One of the most odd observations is that the Bible, which was spoken and written for, by, and to the leadership or intelligentsia of people who were not fully free, in order to preserve and protect their positions of privilege, is significantly utilized by the power brokers in our society in order to preserve and protect their positions of privilege. It is most interesting that the Bible, which is the traditions of a dominated people, is employed by persons who are in power in order to dominate others. In this light, the primary concern with survival forces us as modern readers of the Bible to confront, even critique, our confessional and circumstantial stances if we would embrace the faith of the ancient Yahwists.

SUMMARY

The ancient Yahwists and the modern African Americans share several things. First is a common sociopolitical situation: they are minorities, that is, not fully self-determinant. Second, their lives are complicated by the acutely felt need to acquire or fulfill the basic requirements for survival. They seek to realize and secure freedom. If the African Americans are to appropriate ancient Yahwistic faith, it is mandatory for us (or anyone, for that matter) to contextualize the text, that is, interrelate the premises, presuppositions, and principles of the ancient forebears and the predicaments and problems of the modern believers. The Bible itself models what must be done: the issues of survival must be realistically addressed in the pursuit of freedom. We must describe the circumstances of our existence, particularly the sociopolitical aspects, and determine the identity of our supplier(s) of the requirements for survival. We must determine which requirements remain unfulfilled and finally delineate a course of action that seeks their fulfillment. This, I suggest, can be done only by contextualization of the ancient Yahwistic traditions.

NOTES

1. Norman K. Gottwald, *The Hebrew Bible: A Socio-Literary Introduction* (Philadelphia: Fortress, 1985), 202–6; J. Alberto Soggin, *An Introduction to the History of Israel and Judah*, trans. John Bowden (Valley Forge, Pa.: Trinity Press International, 1993), 235–36.

2. Robert B. Coote, *Early Israel: A New Horizon* (Minneapolis: Fortress, 1990), 5, 72, 88–90, 92–93; Gösta W. Ahlström, *The History of Ancient Palestine from the Palaeolithic Period to Alexander's Conquest*, ed. Diana Edelman (JSOTS 146; Sheffield: Sheffield Academic Press, 1993), 285–88; Soggin, 169.

3. Ahlström, 474, 509, 531–39; Soggin, 64–65, 74; Niels Peter Lemche, *Ancient Israel: A New History of Israelite Society* (Sheffield: Sheffield Academic Press, 1995), 139–40.

4. Robert B. Coote and David Robert Ord (*The Bible's First History: From Eden to the Court of David with the Yahwist* [Minneapolis: Fortress, 1989]) argue that J was a social product of urban Israel composed to validate the establishment of the royal house of David, which replaced the less centralized political arrangement of intertribalism in the highlands of Palestine (3, 6, 7, 29–30, 201) and thus is nationalistic, state propaganda (246) with Yahweh as the god of the nation of Israel (250). Once the kingdom of David-Solomon split, the Northern Kingdom or Israel developed its own traditions (i.e., probably returned to the earlier Mosaic/Sinaitic covenant traditions) in order to justify its monarchy. See Robert B. Coote, *In Defense of Revolution: The Elohist History* (Minneapolis: Fortress, 1991); Alan W. Jenks, *The Elohist and North Israelite Traditions* (Missoula, Mont.: Scholars Press, 1977). Coote's thesis is that E originated as a written supplement to J in the court of Jeroboam to justify his revolution against and secession from the Davidic kingdom (2, 13, 17, 19, 61, 63, 67, 69, 75, 90, 92, 94, 95, 96, 98, 101, 103, 107, 112, 114, 119, 120, 121, 139–40). Jenks's thesis is that the E traditions comprise the fragments of an originally continuous and independent epic tradition that was formulated about 922 B.C.E. from the northern Israelite traditions located among the Mushite (Gershonite) or Levitical priesthood, that is, "prophetic-levitical" group, at Shiloh, after the death of Solomon, when the kingdom divided and an independent state in the north was being established, and was designed for cult or covenant renewal and teaching (1 Kings 11:16—12:33; cf. 102, 104, 105, 120).

5. Ahlström, 568–79, 636–38, 665–680; Soggin, 212–14, 216–20, 235–36; Siegfried H. Horn, "The Divided Monarchy," in *Ancient Israel: A Short History from Abraham to the Roman Destruction of the Temple*, ed. Hershel Shanks (Washington, D.C.: Biblical Archaeology Society/Englewood Cliffs, N.J.: Prentice-Hall, 1988), 120–23; James B. Pritchard, ed., *The Ancient Near East*, vol. 1, *Texts and Pictures* (Princeton, N.J.: Princeton University Press, 1958), 195–98.

6. Ahlström, 675–84; Soggin, 244–46.

7. Frank Crüsemann (*The Torah: Theology and Social History of Old Testament Law*, trans. Allan W. Mahnke [Minneapolis: Fortress, 1996]) locates the Book of the Covenant (BC; Exodus 20:22–23:33 = Exodus 34:11–26 + Exodus 21–22, the Jerusalem Code [הַמִּשְׁפָּטִים]) during this time, considering its authors to be the priests of the Jerusalem court (142, 166), who addressed the free individual landowners who headed clans (142, 189), regarding the conflicts between the two population groups and their religions that had ensued since the beginning of Assyrian domination and the competition among the Yahwistic shrines that ensued after the fall of the Northern Kingdom (120, 124, 126, 173–74). Specifically they were concerned with the possible annihilation by the Assyrians (130), the absence of formalized responsibility and power, and the potential inclusion of any free males and aliens from the north (124, 184, 189), which evidently had resulted in lack of sympathy due to animosity, denial of justice to the poor (e.g.,

slavery; 154–59), exertion of pressure by the majority, and domination of justice by money and power (146, 154, 191). BC serves as metanorms and a critical authority that is intended to hinder the activities of the guilty, with a twofold message: justice for the poor should not be perverted by the powerful; and partiality toward the weak in a lawsuit should not occur in court (190–91). This was achieved through radicalization and intensification of the understanding of older texts (128–29), parallel historicization of these texts (i.e., former instructions became/functioned as God's word to the Israelites in the present situation) (129–30), and marginalization (i.e., separation from the non-Yahwistic Canaanites; 130–31). Also, he argues that after 701 B.C.E., when Sennacherib's reduction of Jerusalem and the centralization of all cults that led to the increased significance of Jerusalem and its temple, and the appointment of a king by the people after the murder of Amon (2 Kings 21:24; 23:30; cf. Deuteronomy 17:14–20) had occurred, a resistance/farmers' liberation movement that was led by "the people of the land" [עַם־הָאָרֶץ] seized power from the aristocratic Jerusalem families and drafted the Deuteronomic Code/Laws (D; Deuteronomy 12–26), addressing the free landowners or the Judeans [עַם־הֿאָרֶץ], legitimating their acts (Deuteronomy 16:18; 17:8–13; 2 Kings 11:14, 18; 22:1; 23:31, 36; 212–15, 219, 223, 235, 238, 240, 247, 249, 266, 268–69). They addressed the following concerns: provision of a counter to polyYHWHism (Deuteronomy 6:4); security for social problems, for example, provision for the weak (Deuteronomy 14:22–29; 15:19–22); regulation of behavior in time of war (Deuteronomy 20); and handling of intrafamilial conflicts, that is, curtailment of the rights of the *paterfamilias* (Deuteronomy 21:18–21; 22:13–21,22, 25–29; 25:5–10; 222, 225, 244–45, 252–257). This was done through employment of several themes: the tithes are the inner design of D (207); abolition of the tithe, that is, payment of it every third year to the socially underprivileged groups (i.e., those without land; Deuteronomy 14:22–23; 23:16; 24:6,14; 234); and the central court holds the same dignity as Moses or the Mosaic law book (Deuteronomy 16:18–20; 17:8–13; 19:1–13; 238–40).

    8. For example, see Isaiah 7; 20:1–6; 30:1–5; 31:1–3; see also Amos 2:6–7; 3:10,15; 4:1; 5:7–13; 6:4–6; 7:10–17; 8:4–6; Hosea 2:8,13,17; 4:1–2,8; 6:10; 9:1,9. The beginning of the classical prophets is marked by the debut of Amos and Hosea, is characterized by the assertion of the universalism of Yahweh, and includes control of foreign nations and powers as his instruments of punishment of Israel when they violate the covenant stipulations. Existentially, and somewhat psychologically, these interpretations serve the purpose of preservation of sanity and of promotion of ideological adherence in light of undergoing crises. Gerhard von Rad (*The Message of the Prophets* [New York: Harper & Row, 1962, 1965]) has argued that Yahwistic prophetism as evidenced by the classical prophets is a conservative countermovement to Israelite state. These prophets interpreted the crises to Israel and Judah as Yahweh's judgment upon them. The emergence of this movement is connected with the degeneracy of Yahwism due to syncretism; political autonomy, or systematic emancipation from Yahweh and his offer of protection brought about by the formation of the state (9); oppressive and exploitative economic and social developments; and the rise of the Assyrians (10). Their messages reflected several common factors: rootedness in the basic

sacral traditions of the early period, that is, Yahwistic tribalism; an intensive view into the future (11–12); proclamations of judgment coupled with the beginnings of a new movement toward salvation (12); and spiritual independence and religious immediacy, that is, involvement in the traditions and general religious ideas of their environment (13). See Lemche, *Ancient Israel*, 155–56. Caution must be taken here, for the classical Yahwistic prophets also operated within a pantheistic view in which Yahweh was the supreme god (Isaiah 2:18–20; Jeremiah 1:4–6; 7:9–19,30–31; 9; Ezekiel 8:10–16; Hosea 2:15; 11:2; 13:1–4,14). However, this aspect of the prophets' activity may reflect a change in emphasis of their roles from cultic to sociopolitical affairs (see Samuel E. Balentine, "The Prophet as Intercessor: A Reassessment," *Journal of Biblical Literature* 103 [1984]: 161–73).

9. Bernard Goldstein and Alan Cooper ("The Festivals of Israel and Judah and the Literary History of the Pentateuch," *Journal of the American Oriental Society* 110 [1990]: 19–31) argue that Hezekiah attempted to restore the authentic Judean traditions via commissioning P, a Jerusalemite priest, to revise Rje in the light of Hezekiah's reform program, thereby commissioning the draft of the Priestly traditions of the Pentateuch. The intent of P was to reestablish the authenticity and centrality of the Davidic cult in Jerusalem (30).

10. Ahlström, 689–91, 701–16, 781–803; Soggin, 248–65; Horn, 131–49; Niels Peter Lemche, "Kings and Clients: On Loyalty Between the Ruler and the Ruled in Ancient 'Israel,'" *Semeia* 66 (1994): 119–32, especially 127–29 (n. 5); James B. Pritchard, ed., *The Ancient Near East,* vol. 2, *A New Anthology of Texts and Pictures* (Princeton, N.J.: Princeton University Press, 1975), 112–13.

11. For example, see Jeremiah 24–25, 27–29, 37–38.

12. Ahlström, 814–17, 834–35, 839, 841–43; Soggin, 266–67, 276–80; Gottwald, 428–29, 482–92; James D. Purvis, "Exile and Return," in *Ancient Israel: A Short History from Abraham to the Roman Destruction of the Temple,* ed. Hershel Shanks (Washington, D.C.: Biblical Archaeology Society/Englewood Cliffs, N.J.: Prentice-Hall, 1988), 156–65; Philip R. Davies, *In Search of "Ancient Israel"* (JSOTS 148; Sheffield: Sheffield Academic Press, 1992), especially 87, 90, 92–93; Pritchard, 1:206–8.

13. Ahlström, 894; Gottwald, 439; Soggin, 300–302; Robert B. Coote and Mary P. Coote, *Power, Politics, and the Making of the Bible: An Introduction* (Minneapolis: Fortress, 1990), 86; Lee I. A. Levine, "The Age of Hellenism," in *Ancient Israel: A Short History from Abraham to the Roman Destruction of the Temple,* ed. Hershel Shanks (Washington, D.C.: Biblical Archaeology Society/ Englewood Cliffs, N.J.: Prentice-Hall, 1988), 177–78.

14. Soggin, 329–42; Levine, "The Age of Hellenism," 187–89, 197–204; Gottwald, 447–56. Gottwald notes that during the Maccabean-Hasmonean period the Pharisees, the Essenes, and the Sadducees originated, while the Zealots arose as an offshoot of Pharisaic circles in 6 B.C.E. (449). The major causes for these factions and parties were the realignment of socioeconomic, political, and religious forces started by the attempt to Hellenize Judaism radically; and the reactive emergence of an independent Jewish state that took on a Hellenistic character in spite of its anti-Hellenistic beginnings (450). The basis for this concern

was twofold: the exclusion of Hellenistic religious syncretism by an overwhelming Jewish consensus; and the Jewish consensus for maintenance of a Jewish religion based on the Torah (450). Specifically, the Pharisees and the Essenes originated because of the breach of the separation of religious and civil offices by the Hasmonean political rulers. The Sadducees emerged as a result of being catapulted into positions of power and leadership by the new opportunities for power and wealth that were spawned by the Maccabean war and the Hasmonean expansion (451). Thus a basic rivalry ensued between the Pharisees and the Sadducees, which was intertwined with socioeconomic and political issues, that is, social class positions and perceived self-interests considerably determined how the Jews aligned themselves on the religiopolitical issues (453, 456). The Pharisees were members of a sect that voluntarily and strictly took on themselves "the yoke of the Torah," having a progressive interpretation of Torah via a twofold Law; equal applicability of purity laws; and a negative view of Hellenized politics and culture. The Essenes' posture was the same as the Pharisees but stricter in application of the Torah. They withdrew from society due to its perceived, social, and political evil. The Sadducees were persons of privilege in the priesthood, or in the lay nobility, who combined pro-Hasmonean sympathies with an elitist religious outlook, having a narrow, constructionist interpretation of Torah; a double standard of purity for priests and laity; and a dichotomy of religious and sociopolitical life (453–54). The Sadducees tended to mandate messianic political action in terms of the prevailing, blunt, and cruel forms of international power politics from a traditional religious view, while the Pharisees tended to mandate messianic loyalty to domestic social equality and justice, eschewing the conceits and excesses of power politics, even to the point of endangering political independence, as long as religious purity and freedom of practice were assured from a traditional religious view (455). Note that Levine and Soggin differ with Gottwald regarding the origin of the Essenes. Both regard them as offshoots of the Sadducees. However, Soggin sees them as breaking away from the Sadducees and joining the Hasidim, because of the Jewish concessions to Hellinism (338–39), while Levine sees two additional factions of Sadducees. One group, the adherents of Onias IV, erected a temple in Leontopolis, Egypt, under Ptolemaic auspices to rival the Jerusalem temple under the Hasmoneans in 150 B.C.E. Another group withdrew to the Judean wilderness and formed the Essene sect (198). Certainly it is obvious that the tensions between the Pharisees and the Sadducees resulted in the development of distinct social bases of operation. Here, the Pharisees probably worked out of the synagogues (see Lee I. Levine, "The Nature and Origin of the Palestinian Synagogue Reconsidered," *Journal of Biblical Literature* 115 [1996]: 425–48; Jerome C. Ross, *The Composition of the Holiness Code (Lev. 17–26)* (Ph.D. diss., University of Pittsburgh, 1997 [UMI 9816816], 148–49), while the Sadducees controlled the temple cultus.

15. Soggin, 323–25; Coote and Coote, 90–91; Levine, 183–84; Gottwald, 444–45; see also Paul D. Hanson, *The Dawn of Apocalyptic: The Historical and Sociological Roots of Jewish Apocalyptic Eschatology,* rev. ed. (Philadelphia: Fortress, 1979), 1–31; Gottwald, 582–94. See 1 and 2 Maccabees, Judith, Ecclesiasticus, Daniel, and the works of Josephus.

16. Soggin, 349–50; Shaye J. D. Cohen, "Roman Domination," in *Ancient Israel: A Short History from Abraham to the Roman Destruction of the Temple,* ed. Hershel Shanks (Washington, D.C.: Biblical Archaeology Society/Englewood Cliffs, N.J.: Prentice-Hall, 1988), 205–7; Martin Noth, *The History of Israel,* trans. Peter R. Ackroyd, rev. ed. (New York: Harper & Row, 1958), 422, 425, 435.

17. Cohen, 215–22.

18. Luise Schottroff, "Women as Followers of Jesus in New Testament Times: An Exercise in Social-Historical Exegesis of the Bible," in *The Bible and Liberation: Political and Social Hermeneutics,* rev. ed. of *A Radical Religion Reader,* ed. Norman K. Gottwald (Maryknoll, N.Y.: Orbis, 1983), 418–27. Schottroff sees the Jesus movement in Palestine as a self-help community of poor Jews that fostered equality of the sexes in the context of shared poverty and hope for the impending kingdom of God.

19. See Howard Clark Kee, "Jesus, The King of the Jews," *Explorations* 9, no. 2 (1995): 1–2; David G. Burke, "Translating *Hoi Ioudaioi* in the New Testament," *Explorations* 9, no. 2 (1995): 1–3.

20. Soggin, 350–51; Cohen, 212, 218, 222; see Matthew, Mark, Luke, and John. Also see Günther Bornkamm, *Jesus of Nazareth,* trans. Irene McLuskey and Fraser McLuskey with James M. Robinson (New York: Harper & Row, 1960); John Reumann, *Jesus in the Church's Gospels: Modern Scholarship and the Earliest Sources* (Philadelphia: Fortress, 1968); Geza Vermes, *Jesus the Jew: A Historian's Reading of the Gospels* (Philadelphia: Fortress, 1973); Howard Clark Kee, *Jesus in History: An Approach to the Study of the Gospels,* 2d ed. (New York: Harcourt Brace Jovanovich, 1977).

21. See Jerome C. Ross, *The History of Ancient Israel: A Compilation. The Lectures of Jerome C. Ross, Ph.D.* (n.p., 1999).

22. Texts are written documents for purposes of recording, teaching, or propaganda. Contexts are the given social settings or situations in which persons live and that have sociopolitical, economic, and cultural dimensions. Concepts are ideas, thoughts, or insights that originate within some contexts by means of some personal interaction or happening, historical or natural, and interpretive.

23. See Coote and Coote, cf. ix, x, 8, 11, 18, 28, 34–35, 36–37, 39, 41, 61, 70–73, 75, 78–80, 87, 92–93, 101, 108–9, 112, 123, 128, 135–36, 139, 149–51, 159–61, 162, 164. Coote and Coote correctly contend that the Bible originated as temple scriptures, was the product and the tool of power struggles between the rich or affluent, and was used to legitimate the political or power status/policies promulgated by these rich and powerful. See also Morton Smith, *Palestinian Parties and Politics That Shaped the Old Testament* (London: SCM, 1987); Gottwald, 596–609; Richard Elliott Friedman, *Who Wrote the Bible?* (New York: Harper & Row, 1987).

24. See Smith; Coote and Coote; Douglas A. Knight, "Political Rights and Powers in Monarchic Israel," *Semeia* 66 (1994): 93–117; Lemche, "Kings and Clients."

25. Three general groups emerged in the early history of Israel: clans and tribes, whose family leaders were the *paterfamilias* and the firstborn sons, whose

political construct was tribalism, whose political representatives were the elders and the Yahwistic prophets, whose cult institutions were the local altars and sanctuaries, and whose cultic leaders were the Levitical priesthood; royal dynasties and households, whose family leaders were the kings and their successors, whose political construct was monarchalism, whose political leaders were the kings and the royal courts (i.e., elders, scribes, sages, and prophets), whose cult institutions were temples, and whose cultic personnel were royally appointed or royally approved priests and cultic prophets; and postexilic Judean families, whose leaders were *paterfamilias*, whose political arrangement was colonialism, whose political leaders were appointees or governors selected and installed by the respective overlords, whose cultic institutions were temples and/or synagogues, whose cultic leaders were Aaronite priests, headed by a high priest and ruling over the Levites. According to this scheme the earliest institutions became normative for Israel and subsequently were established as orthodox. Benevolent forms of the monarchy, if they were ever existent, were obviously accepted, though not by all (see the "people of the land" [עַם־הָאָרֶץ] and the Rechabites, 2 Kings 10:15; Jeremiah 35).

26. Though these early institutions were normative, it is to be noted that with all probability an extremely small sector of Yahwists were strictly monotheistic, and this was due to the composite nature of the formulative traditions and the polytheistic and pluralistic backgrounds of the members that eventually formed Israel. In essence, only the Yahwism as practiced by the orthodoxy was possibly strictly monotheistic; the other forms were syncretistic. However, the theoretical arguments for both that were eventually transcribed and transmitted maintained a monotheistic overtone. See Ross, *Composition of the Holiness Code*, 157, n. 40. From study of the Holiness Code (Leviticus 17—26), I have observed the following characteristics of "popular religion": involvement of the elders, or invoking of the clan leaders, as representatives of the populace (Jeremiah 26:11, 16–17); the prevalence of the veneration of the clan deities; the promulgation of the "all-Israelite" view; the elevation of shabbat to an equal status with the tabernacle; the inclusion of the *gêr;* the anthropomorphizing and personalizing of God; and the view of the covenant between Yahweh and Israel as being reciprocal. The latter five characteristics are features of H that show evidence of influence by popular forms of Yahwism. Being priestly popular, H assumes that the elders are leaders but not over priests; advocates the holiness of all Israelites, even the land, but in grades; elevates shabbat to an equal status with the temple; denounces the clan deities (cf. Leviticus 17:7; 19:4,31; 26:1); includes the *gêr* as equal on conditions of compliance; adopts anthropomorphisms in describing Yahweh; and personalizes the covenant between Yahweh and the people of Israel. In this respect, I define Israelite popular religion as an unofficial form of Yahwism that was headed by local leaders, who were not backed by the political overlords or the authorities in power.

27. See Walter Brueggemann, *Old Testament Theology: Essays on Structure, Theme, and Text,* ed. Patrick D. Miller (Minneapolis: Fortress, 1992), 118–49, 137. The tension between Yahwistic tribalism and exilic period is reflected in Brueggemann's polarity "aniconic religion/egalitarian social practice (the combination of which is called 'pain-embracing')" versus "iconic religion/monopolistic

social practice (the combination of which is called 'structure legitimation')," which the text presents as an accommodation of the popular trends by the official tradents, in which the latter maintains an upper hand. See, for example, the understanding of H in Ross, *Composition of the Holiness Code*, 131–46, 147–61.

28. Joseph Blenkinsopp, *Sage, Priest, Prophet: Religious and Intellectual Leadership in Ancient Israel* (Louisville, Ky.: Westminster/John Knox, 1995), 82–83, 135, 138–39, 142–44, 147; Klaus Koch, *The Prophets*, vol. 1, *The Assyrian Period*, trans. Margaret Kohl (Philadelphia: Fortress, 1983), 31; cf. von Rad, *Message of the Prophets*, 9–14, 30–37.

29. Claus Westermann, *Basic Forms of Prophetic Speech*, trans. Hugh Clayton White (Philadelphia: Westminster, 1967), 205–10; von Rad, *Message of the Prophets*, 229–39; cf. Michael De Roche, "Yahweh's *rîb* Against Israel: A Reassessment of the So-Called 'Prophetic Lawsuit' in the Preexilic Prophets," *Journal of Biblical Literature* 102 (1983): 563–74.

30. Koch, 130–32, 138–40.

31. Blenkinsopp, 82–83, 96; also see Ross, *Composition of the Holiness Code*, 148–49.

32. Patrick D. Miller, *Deuteronomy* (Louisville, Ky.: John Knox, 1990), 12–13. Miller lists as features of D: it is Torah, that is, "preached law" or instruction and teaching; frequent reference to "this day" or "today," that is, contemporaneity; use of "we" in the credos and elsewhere (Deuteronomy 6:20–25; 26:5–11); frequent emphatic use of the second-person pronouns; repeated summons to hear; numerous vocatives; appeal to memory as a way of actualizing the past in the present; use of threats and promises to motivate hearers to respond, including a simplistic view of reward and punishment; appeal to the heart and the mind; and use of illustrations. Included with these may be emphasis on the land as the greatest good and endorsement of a limited monarchy.

33. For features of the priestly-popular form, see n. 26.

34. Gerhard von Rad, "The Levitical Sermon in I and II Chronicles (1934)" in *The Problem of the Hexateuch and Other Essays*, trans. E. W. Trueman Dicken (Edinburgh and London: Oliver & Boyd, 1965), 269, 271, 278. Cf. 2 Chronicles 15:2–7; 16:7–9; 19:6–7,9–11; 20:20; 25:7–8,9b; 28:2–10; 30:6–9; 32:7–8a.

35. Ross, *Composition of the Holiness Code*, 147.

36. See Renita J. Weems, "Reading Her Way Through the Struggle: African American Women and the Bible," in *Stony the Road We Trod: African American Biblical Interpretation*, ed. Cain Hope Felder (Minneapolis: Fortress, 1991), 62; cf. William H. Myers, "The Hermeneutical Dilemma of the African American Biblical Student," in *Stony the Road We Trod*, 52–55. Myers includes as sources for pretexts "near-canonical" traditions of a given community. Pretexts, then, are the specific attitudinal or mental lenses by and through which a given community understands reality; context is the social situation (i.e., political affiliation, economic status, education level, ethnic group, believing community) that predisposes one toward reality or the world. Contexts produce pretexts.

CHAPTER 3

PREACHING IN THE CONTEXT OF POVERTY, ECONOMIC MARGINALIZATION, AND THE IDEAL OF SOCIAL JUSTICE

ROBERT WAFAWANAKA

This chapter seeks to defend the thesis that responsible preaching in the context of poverty and economic marginalization must be faithful to the biblical vision of justice and equality by offering a critique of injustice and oppression as demonstrated by ancient Near Eastern, ancient Israelite, and traditional African cultures. Such preaching must uphold the values of justice, economic liberation, sharing, and caring for the needy members of our societies. If preaching in the context of poverty is to be genuine, it must take the Bible seriously.

The general outline followed here begins with a definition of the terms *poverty* and *economic marginalization* in their biblical and global perspectives. This is followed by a discussion of ideals of social justice as exemplified in the three cultures identified above. This section leads to more in-depth analysis of biblical material, especially legal and prophetic texts. To conclude the discussion, I will focus on the relevance and appeal of African ideals of social justice and morality in light of our topic.

In this chapter, the terms *poverty* and *economic marginalization* are used to refer to material poverty or the lack of sufficient economic resources to afford one a decent standard of living. This usage is in line with the biblical perspective. While a few texts speak of spiritual poverty, the majority of biblical texts on poverty speak about real or economic poverty. Such an approach is also relevant to our own societies. When we speak of poverty from a global perspective, we are inevitably talking about the real poverty that millions of people in this world are experiencing. What

40

is even more startling is the fact that such poverty knows no geographical, religious, or racial bounds. In today's world, poverty exists not only in poor societies but also in affluent societies.

The phenomenon of poverty is neither new nor peculiar to our times. Poverty existed from prebiblical and biblical periods to our own times. Poverty is a timeless problem that consequently requires utmost attention by all human beings. Through the ages, there have been many attempts to address this timeless problem. The appeal to the ideal of social justice is but one way to address this issue with the hope of alleviating the existence of poverty in human societies.

Ideals of social justice are exemplified in the cultures of the ancient Near East and traditional Africa. Classic examples of social justice concern are found especially in the ancient cultures of Egypt, Babylon, and Canaan (Ugarit). In these cultures, the weaker members of society such as widows, fatherless children, resident aliens, and the poor are cared for and protected by either the god or the king, the divine representative on earth.[1] According to F. Charles Fensham, "The protection of widow, orphan, and the poor was the common policy of the ancient Near East."[2] An Egyptian text called the "Instruction for King Merikare" is a didactic text in which the king advises his son and successor on the art of proper rule and the duty expected of the good king:

> Do justice, then you endure on earth;
> Calm the weeper, don't oppress the widow,
> Don't expel a man from his father's property,
> Don't reduce the nobles in their possessions,
> Beware of punishing wrongfully,
> Do not kill, it does not serve you.[3]

Comparatively, Babylonian literature also demonstrates much concern for social justice, especially in the legal and wisdom texts. This sentiment is echoed in the prologue and epilogue of the Law Code of Hammurabi (1728–1686 B.C.E.). The gods commissioned Hammurabi:

> To cause justice to prevail in the land,
> . . . .
> In order that the strong might not oppress the weak,

> that justice might be dealt the orphan (and) the widow,
> . . . .
> to give justice to the oppressed.[4]

Finally, two Ugaritic texts demonstrate that kings were expected to care for the underprivileged. In the legend of King Keret, his son attempts to dethrone him by accusing him of abandoning his royal duties:

> You do not judge the cases of widows,
> You do not preside over the hearings of the oppressed;
> You do not drive out those who plunder the poor,
> You do not feed the orphan before you,
> The widow behind your back.[5]

The second Ugaritic text (Tale of Aqhat) depicts King Daniel (Danel) as sitting at the gate, the traditional ancient Near Eastern seat of justice, judging cases. According to this text, Daniel "judged the cases of widows, presiding over orphans' hearing."[6] These few texts indicate that the ideal of social justice was something that ancient cultures sought to achieve. These ideals are still relevant for us.

Scholars agree that social justice concern in Israel originates in ancient Near Eastern cultures.[7] A survey of the three cultures identified above indicates that the issue of social justice was a prominent one. Ancient Egypt had a distinct notion of law and justice embodied in the concept of *maat*. *Maat* was also the name of a goddess who symbolized "cosmic order and universal harmony established by the gods from the beginning, and represented by the Pharaoh. Only by conforming to *maat* could individuals and the community hope to prosper."[8] Due to the existence of a flourishing life in the hereafter in ancient Egypt, the well being of an individual was also an element of concern after death. In the "Protestation of Guiltlessness" or the so-called Negative Confession, the deceased in the Egyptian Book of the Dead confesses his or her innocence: "I have neither increased or diminished the grain measure. I have not added to the weight of the balance."[9] The greatest number of texts on social concern in antiquity come from Mesopotamia. Specific examples can be found in the reformatory measures of Urukagina, king of Lagash (2300 B.C.E.); the Law Codes of Ur-Nammu, founder of the Third Dynasty of Ur, Lipit-Ishtar of Isin, and Eshnunna. The most enduring example from those ancient times is the Code of Hammurabi, whose 282 laws are sandwiched between the prologue and the epilogue.[10] Unlike ancient Mesopotamia and Egypt, evidence of social concern in Canaan is scant and limited to the Keret and Aqhat texts cited above. This background is the basis of Israelite ideals of social justice.

Due to the extensive nature of social concern in ancient Israel, Paul D. Hanson correctly observes that "contrary to popular opinion, the ancient Israelites did not invent social concern for the welfare of the vulnerable persons like the widow, and the orphan."[11] In light of this evidence, it is easier to comprehend biblical materials. Biblical ideals of social justice concern are expressed in the care and treatment of the poor and other disadvantaged members of the community such as widows, fatherless children, resident aliens, laborers, peasant farmers, and beggars. This care and concern is evident in all the parts of the Hebrew Bible or Old Testament (The Law/Torah, the Prophets, and the Writings), but especially in first two parts.

Social justice concern is enshrined in the three legal codes in the Torah: the Covenant Code (Exodus 20:22–23:33), the Deuteronomic Code (Deuteronomy 12–26), and the Holiness Code (Leviticus 17–26). The Covenant Code expresses Yahweh's care and concern for the welfare of the vulnerable members of society:

> You shall not wrong or oppress a resident alien, for you were aliens in the land of Egypt. You shall not abuse any widow or orphan. If you do abuse them, when they cry out to me, I will surely heed their cry; my wrath will burn, and I will kill you with the sword, and your wives shall become widows and your children orphans. (Exodus 22:21–24)[12]

The Covenant Code also has many other laws addressing different issues relating to poverty and the ideal of social justice. This law code is regarded as the earliest code such that the other two codes contain similar laws that are subsequently developed or transformed. For example, the Covenant Code simply states that if a creditor takes a neighbor's garment as a pledge, that garment should be returned before sunset in order for the poor person to be warm at night (Exodus 22:26–27). This law is expanded in the Deuteronomic Code that forbids the creditor from entering the house of the debtor for the express purpose of taking a pledge item. The text specifically states that "you shall wait outside, while the person to whom you are making the loan brings the pledge out to you" (Deuteronomy 24:11). This requirement was intended to maintain the dignity of the poor person in what was already a humiliating situation.[13] Significantly, Deuteronomy prohibits the seizure of a widow's garment as a pledge (24:17). In general, Deuteronomy has a more humanitarian and socially oriented attitude toward the poor and underprivileged than does Exodus. In the Deuteronomic Code, the resident alien, the fatherless, and the widow are constantly mentioned together as persons in need of communal assistance. During the harvest festival, the forgotten sheaf, some of the beaten olives, and gleaned grapes are to be left behind for their sustenance (Deuteronomy 24:19–21; cf. Leviticus 19:9–10; 23:22). Furthermore, Deuteronomy implies that all debts are to be canceled every seven years and the poor should not really exist if only Israel obeys the law of God and takes care of its poor (Deuteronomy 15:1–11).

The ideal of social justice is also carried on by the Holiness Code. The prime example in this code is the jubilee text of Leviticus 25:8–55, which is preceded by a discussion of the sabbatical year in 25:1–8. The jubilee year, which came in approximately the fiftieth year, was a classic example of Israelite concern and provision for the poor. During the year of jubilee, the law stated that liberty was to be proclaimed throughout the land of Israel, debt slaves were to be released, and land and property were to be returned to their original owners. The law not only provided economic stability for the poor but also reunited families that had been separated because of the burden of debt. While biblical scholars largely doubt that jubilee was ever practiced,[14] we should not lose sight of the ideal itself and the high principle it represents. Such a principle is one that faithful preaching ought to uphold. This principle is also reflected in the prophetic paradigm that is worth emulating.

The great prophets of ancient Israel who were the major advocates of the poor can inform responsible preaching in the context of poverty, economic marginalization, and the ideal of social justice. Minor prophets such as Amos and Micah, and major prophets like Isaiah and Jeremiah, are cases in point. These prophets were not afraid to proclaim the message of Yahweh to the nation of Israel and its rulers. This message was timely due to the injustice of Israel's neglect and oppression of the poor, especially at those times, such as the eighth century B.C.E., that the nation was very prosperous. The prophets, especially those identified above, appear to us as the champions of justice and the economic liberation of the poor.

Amos, the first of the writing prophets, leaves us a legacy of fearlessness to criticize authority when confronted by a great miscarriage of justice in Israelite society. Although a southerner, he travels north to deliver the message of Yahweh. He attacks the Israelites "because they sell the righteous for silver, and the needy for a pair of sandals" (Amos 2:6; 8:4,6). In essence, they are practicing debt slavery for the smallest of debts. Amos also takes issue with the lack of justice for the poor in the legal system designed to protect them (Amos 2:7; 5:12,15). Apparently being aware of Israel's legal tradition, Amos is revolted that the law concerning the garment taken in pledge was being flagrantly abused in the holiest of places (Amos 2:8; cf. Exodus 22:26–27; Deuteronomy 24:10–13). He sarcastically refers to the oppressive women of Samaria as "cows of Bashan" (Amos 4:1). From our perspective, Amos commits an act of treason when he criticizes King Jeroboam II and pronounces that he will die and the nation will be exiled (Amos 7:11). This bold utterance leads to his expulsion from Israel by Amaziah the priest of Bethel (Amos 7:12–13). If Amos were a preacher, there is no doubt that the heart of his message would lie in these beautifully poetic words:

> But let justice roll down like waters,
>> and righteousness like an everflowing stream. (Amos 5:24)

The prophet Micah is also appalled by the oppression of the poor during his time. He describes their oppression in revolting cannibalistic language. The evildoers flay the skin off the people; they eat it; they break the bones and boil them (Micah 3:1–3). The rulers "abhor justice and pervert all equity" and build Jerusalem "with blood and...with wrong" (Micah 3:9–10). In a manner reminiscent of Amos, Micah reiterates that what the Lord requires is simply "to do justice, and to love kindness, and to walk humbly with your God" (Micah 6:8).

This, too, would be the message of Micah if he were a preacher. Although Isaiah, a contemporary of Micah, was probably part of the political establishment,[15] he was also not afraid to speak against injustice, poverty, and oppression. In an allegory of the vineyard describing the relationship between Yahweh and Israel, he reveals the disappointing results: "He expected justice, but saw bloodshed; righteousness, but heard a cry" (Isaiah 5:7). Isaiah also attacks those who practice latifundia (Isaiah 5:8); design unjust laws (Isaiah 10:1); oppress the poor, the widow, and the fatherless (Isaiah 10:2); and practice injustice in the courts of law (Isaiah 29:20–21). Once again, I believe that if Isaiah were a preacher, the following text would resonate with his audience if he were preaching in the context of poverty and economic misery:

> Is not this the fast that I choose:
>> to loose the bonds of injustice,
>> to undo the thongs of the yoke,
> to let the oppressed go free,
>> and to break every yoke?
> Is it not to share your bread with the hungry,
>> and bring the homeless poor into your house;
> when you see the naked, to cover them,
>> and not to hide yourself from your own kin?...
> If you offer your food to the hungry
>> and satisfy the needs of the afflicted,
> then your light shall rise in the darkness
>> and your gloom be like the noonday. (Isaiah 58:6–10)

Like Amos, Micah, and Isaiah, the prophet Jeremiah was concerned about social justice issues in his prophecy. Jeremiah is challenged by Yahweh to run through the streets of Jerusalem and find only one just person (Jeremiah 5:1).[16] To his amazement, the prophet finds only much corruption and wickedness as well as the oppression of the poor and the fatherless (Jeremiah 5:27–28). He adds, "There is nothing but oppression within her [Jerusalem]" (Jeremiah 6:6). Through his fearless criticisms, Jeremiah has created many enemies who seek his own life. Upon these enemies he places a most devastating curse in a personal lament. He wishes that his enemies and their children die so that their wives may become childless and widowed (Jeremiah 18:19–21). Jeremiah even admonishes the king to treat the resident alien, fatherless, and widow in a just manner (Jeremiah 22:1–5). He criticizes two kings of Judah, the sons of Josiah (the beloved king of Judah), for not walking in their father's way (Jeremiah 22:11–23). Josiah won praise for judging the cause of the poor and needy (Jeremiah 22:16).

In the so-called temple sermon (Jeremiah 7:1–15; 26:1–6), Jeremiah indeed acts like a preacher by delivering a devastating attack from the temple court. He essentially argues that it is both deceptive and hypocritical to say "this is the temple of the LORD" when in fact the resident alien, the fatherless, and the widow are being oppressed (Jeremiah 7:4–6). The temple only offers them a false sense of security. Hence Jeremiah warns them: "Amend your ways and your doings" (Jeremiah 7:3).

These examples serve to illustrate that when one preaches in the context of poverty, economic need, and the ideal of social justice, he or she has a wealth of material upon which to base the sermon in order for it to be effective. A tradition of care, concern, and support for the poor is evident in ancient Near Eastern and biblical literature. The preacher therefore stands on solid ground from which to deliver the sermon. The situation of the African American preacher is further strengthened by another basis that is more immediate. This is the African tradition and culture out of which the African American preacher emerges.

African ideals of social justice and morality are captured in the way in which African religion, society, and culture function. Religion and culture set the tone to understanding African philosophy and beliefs. According to John Mbiti, "Africans are notoriously religious.... Religion permeates into all the departments of life so fully that it is not easy or possible always to isolate it."[17] Therefore, in African philosophy, the distinction between the sacred and the secular does not exist. These notions are two sides of the same coin.

African tradition posits that persons do not have individual existence outside of the group. People rejoice and suffer together such that "whatever happens to the individual happens to the whole group, and whatever happens to the whole group happens to the individual."[18] This sense of corporate existence is strengthened by African kinship structures. Generally speaking, Africans are related to each other by blood, betrothal, totem, or communal existence. Mbiti plainly and clearly states this fact when he says, "Everybody is related to everybody else."[19]

Other cultural values of African peoples are their hospitable nature, communal spirit, and desire to share with others. Writing about the Yoruba of Nigeria, E. Bolaji Idowu states, "The Yoruba are by nature a hospitable race and are particularly hospitable to strangers.... The Yoruba teach that one should be hospitable because it is right to be so."[20] Although Idowu's study focuses on a particular group, his observations apply to many African people. With regard to the idea of sharing, Africans cherish sharing the little that they have with others, especially strangers. These communal attitudes obviously relativize the effects of poverty on individuals.

In African philosophy, the idea of morality is closely connected to religion. In fact, Idowu calls morality "the fruit of religion."[21] While Africans worship God through their ancestors, the object of worship is God himself. This fact has often been misconstrued to mean that Africans worship ancestors. Nothing could be further from the truth. Mbiti gives a succinct description of African morality: "The essence of African morality is that it is more 'societary' than 'spiritual'; it is a morality of 'conduct' rather than a morality of 'being...it defines what a person *does* rather than what he *is*.'"[22] This definition of African morality is closely tied to the notions of corporate personality and hospitality.

Another cultural value of Africans is the family, whose combined strength can be used to confront any problem. In fact the African concept of family is much wider than the Western notion of the family, which tends to include only the nuclear family. The African family is an extended family whose members include parents, children, grandparents, uncles, aunts, nephews, nieces, cousins, and in-laws. Mbiti adds to this circle by including the unborn and the deceased whom he refers to as "the living-dead."[23] The natural strength that exists in such large numbers is a force to reckon with in the face of adversity. John Iliffe sheds much light on this fact by stating that "families were and are the main sources of support for the African poor."[24] This datum is significant in that despite the efforts of colonial governments in Africa, the family sustained its members through difficult times. By contrast, Iliffe's research shows how colonialism created its own categories of the poor in addition to the traditional poor. It is therefore evident that African tradition, religion, morality, society, culture, and family structure all contribute to the alleviation of poverty and the lessening of its otherwise devastating consequences. In these concepts lie the values of social solidarity, communal responsibility, mutual support, sharing, and caring for the less fortunate members of our societies. For the one who performs a preaching task in the midst of poverty, I believe that these values can be of significant help. In particular, the African American preacher stands within this rich tradition. He or she can derive some useful paradigms with which to confront the subject of poverty from the pulpit. The combination of ancient Near Eastern, biblical, and African attitudes toward poverty and the ideals of social justice endow the preacher with a rich and extensive legacy, as well as a platform from which to preach effectively.

Many African American preachers have taken advantage of this diverse legacy. Henry H. Mitchell argues that black preaching was influenced by African and other cultures. He writes: "Black preaching and Black religion were greatly influenced by the confluence of two streams of culture, one West African and the other Euro-American."[25] As such the black approach to the Bible is characterized by the use of oral tradition, African wisdom materials, creativity, imagination, and viewing the Bible as one's story.[26] Mitchell also stresses that black preaching is characterized by a particular type of language and expression peculiar to black people. This is the language and culture of the people, the black vernacular. This "Black language," Mitchell argues, is "the rich rendition of English spoken in the Black ghetto."[27]

Indeed, Dr. Martin Luther King Jr. exemplifies what preaching in the context of poverty, economic marginalization, and the ideal of social justice ought to aspire toward. No one who has ever listened to his "I Have a Dream" speech can be unmoved by his sheer eloquence. Like the prophets of ancient Israel, Dr. King was a modern prophet who was not afraid to criticize injustice and oppression. In the "Letter from Birmingham Jail," Dr. King boldly declares: "Injustice anywhere is a threat to justice everywhere."[28] Like a modern Amos or Jeremiah, Dr. King asserts that black people had suffered oppression and injustice long enough that their freedom could no longer be delayed. He cites Jesus, Luther, Jefferson, and others as "extremists" for standing their ground for the truth. In prophetic fashion, Dr. King declares that "justice too long delayed is justice denied."[29] Preaching in the context of poverty means not only addressing the poor and their situation; it also means confronting the political and social structures that create poverty in the first place.

An equally prominent African American preacher, Samuel D. Proctor, argues that preaching the gospel in the context of community crises involves the application of "prophetic insight" in "uncomfortable situations."[30] Proctor eloquently describes how responsible preaching in context ought to be: "The Bible endows the preacher with a passion for justice and with compassion for the victims of injustice; it gives the preacher the penetrating vision to see the eternal hand of God at work in the midst of our contemporaneity."[31] In light of these circumstances, Proctor recommends three priorities — eliminating poverty amid plenty; education; and family stability.[32]

Responsible preaching in the context of poverty requires the preacher to possess a prophetic spirit. J. Philip Wogaman describes one of his ten principles of prophetic preaching (hope) as follows:

> Prophetic preaching deals not only with problems and evils to be overcome; it offers hope that they *can* be overcome. This was the hallmark of most of the great biblical prophets, and it has been a striking contribution of

the African American pulpit. No matter how wretched the situation may be, no matter how powerful the forces of evil that confront us, no matter how futile all aspirations may seem — still, nevertheless, it is God's world, so there is always hope.[33]

While prophetic preaching offers hope to the oppressed hearers of the word, it also provides a challenge to the oppressors to whom the message may be directed.

The challenge of prophetic preaching is especially evident in the context of oppression. In an essay on "An Ante-bellum Sermon," David T. Shannon illustrates this dilemma. Preachers during the period of slavery often addressed the existential situation of slaves but in a veiled or cryptic way in order to avoid alarming the slave owner. The poetic "Ante-bellum Sermon" by Dunbar illustrates how preachers used the methods of "contextuality," "correlation," "confrontation," and "consolation" to successfully address both the oppressed and the oppressors.[34]

While preaching to the powerful or oppressors is risky business, it nevertheless is something that must be done and done correctly. Ronald J. Sider and Michael A. King warn that "to preach in such a context *is* at times to offer not balm but saving grace. It is to proclaim that...some hard choices will have to be made....It is to remind people that when God breaks in and Jesus comes, life does not go on as usual but gets turned upside down."[35]

In this chapter I have attempted to demonstrate that responsible preaching in the context of poverty, economic marginalization, and the ideal of social justice is a challenging task fraught with potential problems. In order to be effective, the preacher must stand solidly on biblical ground. He or she must possess a prophetic spirit that will enable him or her to proclaim the word to both poor and rich without any reservations. If the preacher is African American, he or she inherits a rich and extensive legacy of preaching within the milieu of African cultures and traditions, the experiences of African Americans in America, Western cultural values, and strong biblical grounding that has its antecedents in the larger and older cultures of the ancient Near East.

Responsible preaching in the context of poverty must present a God of justice and equality, a God willing to take nations to task for their neglect of the poor. Preaching must also uphold the values of community, family unity, and social solidarity. Faithful preaching ought to apply the biblical message to our contemporary situation to determine its relevance. It must indicate how we can appropriate the paradigms of social justice and equality that we find in ancient Near Eastern, ancient Israelite, and traditional African cultures. As demonstrated by prophets like Amos, Micah, Isaiah, and Jeremiah, responsible preaching must maintain the same message, whether it is preached in the context of poverty and economic deprivation or that of affluence and material well-being. Finally, preaching in the context of poverty and economic deprivation requires the preacher to address the situation of the poor concretely and offer them hope, possess the courage to challenge the status quo, and be prepared to suffer the consequences of such a message to those who would otherwise benefit from the proliferation of a situation of poverty and economic marginalization.

Notes

1. See the excellent essay by F. Charles Fensham, "Widow, Orphan, and the Poor in Ancient Near Eastern Legal and Wisdom Literature," *Journal of Near Eastern Studies* 21 (1962): 129–39, and also Richard D. Patterson, "The Widow, the Orphan, and the Poor in the Old Testament and the Extra-Biblical Literature," *Bibliotheca Sacra* 130 (July–September 1973): 223–34.

2. Fensham, 129.

3. Miriam Lichtheim, *Ancient Egyptian Literature*, vol. 1 (Berkeley, Los Angeles, and London: University of California Press, 1973), 108. See also James B. Pritchard, ed., *Ancient Near Eastern Texts Relating to the Old Testament*, 3rd ed. (Princeton, N.J.: Princeton University Press, 1969), 415; henceforth cited as *ANET*.

4. *ANET*, 164, 178.

5. Michael David Coogan, ed. and trans., *Stories from Ancient Canaan* (Louisville, Ky.: Westminster, 1978), 74. See also *ANET*, 149.

6. Coogan, 35, 40–41. See also *ANET*, 151, 153.

7. Bruce V. Malchow, *Social Justice in the Hebrew Bible: What Is New and What Is Old?* (Collegeville, Minn.: Liturgical Press, 1996), 1–7; Paul D. Hanson, "The Ancient Near Eastern Roots of Social Welfare," in *Through the Eye of a Needle: Judeo-Christian Roots of Social Welfare*, ed. Emily Albu Hanawalt and Carter Lindberg (Kirksville, Mo.: The Thomas Jefferson University Press at Northeast Missouri State University, 1994), 7–28.

8. Hanson, 14.

9. *ANET*, 34.

10. Malchow, 1–3; Hanson, 9–11; *ANET*, 163–77.

11. Hanson, 9. See also Malchow, who argues that Israel adopted, adapted, or transformed ancient Near Eastern ideals (6, 76–78).

12. All biblical citations are from the New Revised Standard Version (NRSV).

13. Leslie J. Hoppe, "Deuteronomy and the Poor," *The Bible Today* 24 (1986): 373.

14. See Roland de Vaux, *Ancient Israel: Its Life and Institutions*, trans. John McHugh (New York, Toronto, and London: McGraw-Hill, 1961), 177; León Epsztein, *Social Justice in the Ancient Near East and the People of the Bible* (London: SCM, 1986), 134; and Robert K. Gnuse, "Jubilee Legislation in Leviticus: Israel's Vision of Social Reform," *Biblical Theology Bulletin* 15, no. 2 (1985): 47.

15. See Robert R. Wilson, *Prophecy and Society in Ancient Israel* (Philadelphia: Fortress, 1980), 271–73.

16. This is reminiscent of Abraham's wager with Yahweh in Genesis 18:23–33.

17. John S. Mbiti, *African Religions and Philosophy*, 2d rev. and enl. ed. (Oxford: Heinemann, 1990), 1.

18. Ibid., 106.

19. Ibid., 102, 103.

20. E. Bolaji Idowu, *Olódùmarè: God in Yoruba Belief* (London: Longmans, 1962), 157. The latter argument is what ethicists refer to as a deontological argument because it is "absolutist" and "one cannot argue beyond [it]." See Robin Gill, *A Textbook of Christian Ethics* (Edinburgh: T & T Clark, 1985), 5–6, 157–60.

21. Idowu, 145. Kofi A. Opoku supports Idowu's claim by remarking that morality originates from religion, is pervasive in African culture, and the two cannot be separated from each other. See *West African Traditional Religion* (Accra: FEP, 1978), 152–53.

22. Mbiti, *African Religions and Philosophy*, 209 (Mbiti's emphasis). See also Mbiti's *Introduction to African Religion*, 2d ed. (London: Heinemann, 1991), 174–79.

23. Mbiti, *African Religions and Philosophy*, 81–89.

24. John Iliffe, *The African Poor: A History* (Cambridge: Cambridge University Press, 1987), 7.

25. Henry H. Mitchell, *Black Preaching: The Recovery of a Powerful Art* (Nashville: Abingdon, 1990), 30.

26. Ibid., chap. 4.

27. Ibid., 78; see also 15, 20, 81–83. To illustrate the point, Mitchell observes: "The cadences of the late Dr. Martin Luther King, Jr., were unashamedly Black" (82).

28. Martin Luther King Jr., *Why We Can't Wait* (New York and Scarborough, Ontario: New American Library, 1964), 77.

29. Ibid., 81.

30. Samuel D. Proctor, *Preaching About Crises in the Community* (Philadelphia: Westminster, 1988), 18.

31. Ibid., 43–44.

32. Ibid., 81–91. Proctor concludes that preaching is meaningless if it does not address the real needs of the congregation (ibid., 116, 129). David H. C. Read agrees with this assertion when he writes: "If none of our sermons ever offers a hint that we are daily in contact with real people, daily sharing their experiences, and available for serious conversations that go beyond the chitchat of a coffee hour, then the Word is not being truly preached." See *Preaching About the Needs of Real People* (Philadelphia: Westminster, 1988), 26. H. Beecher Hicks bluntly states that the preacher who does not understand the political realities of the church is either a hopeless optimist or an incurable fool. See *Preaching Through a Storm* (Grand Rapids, Mich.: Zondervan, 1987), 183.

33. J. Philip Wogaman, *Speaking the Truth in Love: Prophetic Preaching to a Broken World* (Louisville, Ky.: Westminster/John Knox, 1998), 82. For the other nine principles, see 74–85. Wogaman adds that every preacher must aim to be a prophet, pastor, and an evangelist. As a result, a truly prophetic sermon often leads to opposition regardless of how good the pastor is (10, 19).

34. See David T. Shannon, " 'An Ante-bellum Sermon': A Resource for an African American Hermeneutic," in *Stony the Road We Trod: African American Biblical Interpretation*, ed. Cain Hope Felder (Minneapolis: Fortress, 1991), 98–123. According to Brian K. Blount, this is a "New Hermeneutic" that, by addressing the urgent needs of the congregation, is of "sociopolitical import." See *Cultural Interpretation: Reorienting New Testament Criticism* (Minneapolis: Fortress, 1995), 75.

35. Ronald J. Sider and Michael A. King, *Preaching About Life in a Threatening World* (Philadelphia: Westminster, 1987), 111. See also the essays in *A New Look at Preaching*, ed. John Burke (Wilmington, Del.: Michael Glazier, 1983).

CHAPTER 4

THE SERMON AS
A SUBMITTED STATEMENT

MILES JEROME JONES

In their newsletter of July 1999, *The Mitchell Update*, Ella and Henry Mitchell express gratitude for the outstanding number of awards and honors both have received in the past two years. As one who has appreciated their ministry for almost three decades, I say the recognition is a testimony of appreciation that is well deserved. Few persons have contributed to the library of preaching material as Henry Mitchell has done from the positions of pastor and academician. His writings have challenged black and white homileticians as well as inspired countless parishioners across the years.

Although I have been a student of much of his writing since the 1970s, recent experience has taught me to appreciate the substantive approach to personal application that Mitchell constantly stresses. He encourages preachers to remember that the sermon is a "creature of the people" and therefore in need of being restored to the realm of experiential embrace. In *The Recovery of Preaching* this observation is dealt with at length, and in the book's postscript I find a summarizing statement that launches this chapter. It is set forth in the simple sentence that concludes: "The recovery of preaching will occur only when it comes back to the people."[1] I find these words to be challenging and provocative. There is suggested in them a desirability for a resumed relationship between the essence of the biblical story and the experiences of the people who hear the scriptural words. It seems to me that this is a reminder that preaching is for the people whereas it is often viewed and taught as a vehicle for the preacher. Of course, there are skills to be acquired if one is to effectively present sermonic content, but the emphasis in much of the homiletics curriculum seems to minimize what Mitchell calls the "behavioral objective" of the sermon's intent.

There is a servant motif and a submission to scrutiny to be remembered if preaching is to be appreciated by those who are expected to heed its admonitions or be buoyed by its helpful proclamation. The biblical word is the authoritative servant of the church even as the pastor or preacher is the servant of the parishioners to whom he or she ministers. This recognition allows us to focus on functions of preachment, which can be called the servant sermon. As such, it is an instrument based on biblical authority delivered out of one's own experience with the Word and designed to address a similar experience in the hearer. Method, type, and structure become secondary considerations. Primary interest is found in the possibilities that the instrumentality of the sermon provides a vehicle for change in the actions of the listener. Like a tool similar to a hammer in a carpenter's hand, the sermon awaits the initiative of another before its fulfillment can be realized. In and of itself, the sermon is no more or less than a submitted statement, yielded as the preacher's declaration for reception and response by another.

Much of the significance of a sermon is determined by that to which it is yielded. Action that best suits our sermon preparation and delivery is that which shows itself to have been submitted to the influence of more than a desire for exalted verbal expression or rhetoric. For the purpose of the parish, this means engaging in sermon effort that is directed toward the task of affecting the daily practices of people. Therefore, in addition to sermons being biblically based and exegetically explored, they also need to be experientially attuned. The sermon as statement is a declaration by deed as well as an oral allegation. Thus the authority and influence to which the preacher has turned for final governance are determinative factors for preparation, delivery, and reception of the proclamation. P. T. Forsyth, that venerable philosopher and theologian, reminded us:

> A true sermon is a real deed. It puts the preacher's personality into an act. That is the chief form of Christian life and practice. And one of his great difficulties is that he has to multiply words about what is essentially a deed.... The Gospel means something done and not simply declared.[2]

Christian preaching of that gospel is very much a matter of acknowledging that the assertions made have been subjected to some aspect of what emanates from the life, death, and resurrection of Jesus as the Christ. Inasmuch as that content is critical to the determination of our sermons, it is fitting and proper that we see Jesus as the model for our own preaching. As our model of that to which the sermon is to be submitted, we turn to Jesus' own sermon following his wilderness experience as indicated in the Gospel of Luke. "Why Luke?" one might ask. Surely there are numerous places in the Gospels where one might turn for a sample of Jesus' sermonic submission. Perhaps, but recent scholarship has shown that one of the purposes of Luke's Gospel might be associated with its sermonic character. Robert J. Karris describes Luke as a "kerygmatic story that is meant to preach to the reader in narrative form and elicit from the reader an act of Christian faith."[3] It can be claimed, then, that one purpose of the Lukan narrative is to submit a statement of one's faithful regard for the Christ to another, namely, Theophilus, for the purpose of his believing acceptance. As recorded in Luke 4:14–30, that sermon shows itself to have been governed by several factors that we would do well to note.

It is a sermon delivered under the influence of the power of the Spirit. This episode in Luke helps our understanding of the phenomenal necessity for having a spiritual presupposition attend the utterances of those who would speak a word of truth to the circumstances of their times. Having previously given himself to the influence and leading of the One whom he called Father, Jesus thus enters the incident of this text already affected by the circumstances of that relationship. Whatever he says and does now is not of himself alone. He will address the unfolding events out of a sense of kinship with the Eternal, and from that relationship he will acknowledge himself to be both empowered and anointed. This can be considered the meaning of verse 14, wherein is noted his return to the territory of Galilee and specifically to the area of Nazareth. He returns to this region "in the power of the Spirit." In other words, Jesus, merely by his coming and going, shows us the best evidence of personal spiritual subjection. He does not wait until he has mounted the pulpit of the synagogue to show the influence that dominates his life.

While he is en route in regions and traveling in territories we are made privy to that which profoundly affected his pronouncements.

The words of the preacher are to be already influenced by and submitted to the presence of the One who has called him or her into service. The presupposition is that those who are chosen for service are sensitive to a designation of the divine. That designation makes one an instrument of God's doing in the world and permits an assertion of spiritual empowerment and anointing, which is exactly what we hear Jesus claiming as he proceeds to preach the sermon. However, before the sermon is preached, we see him as one whose actions are acknowledged to be influenced by a relationship with righteousness characterized as his father's "house" or "business" that he must be in or about (Luke 2:49). We see him, before he preaches, as one who has surrendered to the claim of the Eternal who he understood to be his Father. Thus surrendered, he was strengthened for the intervening incident that led him to the pulpit for pronouncement. It is from Jesus' action that we learn how preaching is very much related to the matter of yielding before the sermon is spoken.

The text of Luke provides another factor that helps us to understand aspects of the sermon as a submitted statement. Jesus' sermon on that occasion provided a glimpse of his self-understanding as related to the words of the prophet Isaiah. It was in light of this prophetic precursor that we hear Jesus express his belief about God's claim upon his life. It is the prophet's words to which he turns for a testimony of himself, and it is under the influence of those words that fulfillment is announced. This action highlights another aspect of that which governs the sermon and denotes something else to which it needs be subjected and submitted, namely, the record of Scripture.

"We preach not ourselves," as the apostle Paul has aptly noted, and we are to be warned against doing so. But also we preach not a mere commentary on current affairs, drawing our texts from the latest edition of newspapers or periodicals. Ours is the task of placing the intended preachment under the aegis of Scripture, which alone is able to withstand the indifference or animosity that our words might provoke.

We take our best thought and lay it under the lamp of God's Word to see where the lines match between what we would say and what God has done. When we find the point of parallel, then we dare to make the pronouncement: "This day is the Scripture fulfilled in your hearing." Moreover, we do not use Scripture in an effort to convince the listener concerning the truth of our proclamation. Our submission to Scripture is for preparation to speak to the will, not the intellect, of the listener. Our resort to Scripture is not as evidence to persuade but as indications to inspire; to identify the life-giving presence of God as it is made manifest in the person of Jesus as the Christ. Having said this, let us return to our model again.

Notice how Jesus resorts to the prophetic record, which for him and his time was Scripture. Then notice how the passage from Isaiah is found, suggesting a questionable degree of expectation in the searching effort — "he found the place" but not in the willingness to appropriate, apply, and announce it as a part of his self-understanding. Jesus thus places himself under the previous word of the prophet. He declares and then dares to become its deed that day, thereby allowing the Scripture to become more than record. Through his action we see Scripture becoming the living will of God through the one who yields to it.

The preacher submits to Scripture as though the whole Word of God were a sermon for his benefit. He does not seek to find a sermon in the Scripture until first the confession is made that he or she has been found by the grace to which the Scriptures point. That grace, while gathered to a personal point in the life of Jesus as the Christ, is nevertheless expressed in multiple places in the whole of Scripture. Creation that goes awry and is nevertheless redeemed shows it. An exodus from bondage, a remnant from captivity, a voice crying in the wilderness; all these and more are but evidence that the unmerited favor of God is to be found with a faithfulness to which the preacher can submit. In addition, the whole principle of scriptural necessity is underscored by the preacher's practice. We rely upon the Word and yield our intentions to its dictates because it stands as our representative of authority in the best sense of that word. It is not the Scripture superimposed upon our thought, stifling and narrowing our vision to literal expression alone. Rather, it is Scripture as that enlarging, augmenting factor, permitting and creating a guided imagination that would be made less credible in the absence of scriptural stimulation and authority. Yielded to Scripture, the sermon can embrace imagination based on the formula "inasmuch as" while avoiding the speculation that is too often begun with "let us suppose."

Sermons that are seriously submitted to Scripture not only avoid damaging speculation but are better able to encompass historical relevancy as well and thereby prevent our preaching from becoming vague sentimentalism. Scriptural grounding gives us historical bases vital for Christian preaching. Here I must make an acknowledgment that one of the reasons this Lukan account of Jesus' return to his home district appeals to me is because of my belief in the importance of the historical nitty-gritty symbolism of Nazareth. No matter how cosmic the Christ we are finally called upon to proclaim, he is at first grounded in the Bible's history of his homeland. Scripture signifies that it is by way of Nazareth that he comes to us, and our statements about him need to be submitted to that reality. It is by way of Nazareth and what Nazareth stands for that he is born anew into the life of each one who is born again.

When we return to the Scripture text, we find the concluding aspect to which the sermon is submitted, and that is to the scrutiny of the listeners. There is a perilous problem to which every preacher's sermons are subjected, and Jesus' declarations were no different if we are to believe this account in Luke. That peril is the people who hear the preacher's words. If the preacher's pronouncements were to be privately dispensed as counsel or confidence, the speaker could no doubt be spared much anguish. But the preacher's words must stand the test of public audition and are therefore submitted to a congregation of persons who represent varied and sundry interests and expectations. It is this possibility of peril engendered by the preacher's proclamation that sharpens the dilemma of having the sermon as a statement of submission to public scrutiny — and yet it cannot be avoided. If the sermon were to be only a matter of the preacher's offering to God, for example, then Jesus in this scriptural account could have by-passed the synagogue on that occasion and retired to the solitude of the hills beyond. For perhaps nowhere else in Scripture can we see such a hostile response to his preaching as is here evidenced by the actions of these listeners. Jesus submitted himself to the glare of public presentation, and his words became the cause for a wide expression of emotions ranging from commendation to criticism, from awe to wrath.

This action strikes at the heart of what Mitchell indicates when he insists that preaching must come back to the people. It must run the risk of being submitted to the vagaries of their experience and emotions. Among other things, sermons reflect the recognition of the people's need to be in touch with the Eternal through the Word that is faithfully promulgated. How else will persons be confronted with the will of God except through the Word that is laid out before them as a clear call of challenge or consolation? Neither can we avoid the emotions that might be provoked, as the incident in Luke so amply indicates. Sermons are designed to evoke strong response because their aim is the human will; to be answered not by "I see," as enlightenment, but "I will" or "I will not," as volition. It is possible that parishioners will not like the sermons we preach any more than Jesus' listeners liked his on that occasion. However, because our sermons need to be submitted to public review, it is to be of concern to us that our words at least reflect the basis of our belief that God alone is the final judge of our pronouncements. A major part of the peril to which I refer is due to the fact that the majority of the people to whom we preach do not know the Bible or its awesome appeal to the sinful soul. Something less than the need for love or grace seems to have gripped current consciousness. Even long-time church members go panting after proofs and prosperity these days and seem not to be able to stand the challenge to a faithful risk of relationship with God. They seek a certainty not found in Scripture rather than risk a relationship of discipline and devotion fashioned by the Word of God. Just as Jesus' listeners had no room for considering the Syrian Naaman or the widow of Sidon as acceptable illustrations of God's concern for persons beyond the borders of country or covenant, so do many modern parishioners permit a narrow search for certitude to cause a serious misreading of Scripture that obviates grace and limits love.

There is another aspect of the peril to which such submission points, and that is the fact that one can bask in the superficiality of popular acclaim. How tempting it is to consider that submitting the sermon to the glare of public scrutiny means fashioning a high-sounding statement that might convince the people that this home boy is thoroughly acceptable. However, we learn from this model episode that the sermon, like Jesus' life itself, would be submitted to the people but not controlled by them. It is the action of conveying with concern rather than catering with solicitude.

What then might be the final response to the preacher's need to recognize the fact that the sermon is to be a statement (1) fashioned under the aegis of the Spirit and (2) yielded to the guidance of Scripture, as well as being (3) subject to public scrutiny? While some might blithely ignore these requirements, they do so by missing what Jesus so helpfully demonstrated in the example of Luke 4. We see him not giving a lesson about delivering a sermon as a statement submitted but living out the experience of doing so in an exemplary fashion. Thus we learn, as he always bids us, by following him.

In other words, place our sermons before the people as statements reflecting a faith in the living God whom we ourselves have tried and come to know. Take a text, yes; but know that true biblical preaching is primarily declaring the gospel that is experienced and then using the Bible that is known. We then become those living epistles of whom the apostle Paul spoke, "written on the hearts, to be known and read of all men" (2 Corinthians 3:2). In no sense does that mean our statements will be guaranteed acceptable for those to whom they are submitted. For the only guarantee that goes with sermons is that if they are faithfully set forth as the Word of God and not our words, they shall not return void of accomplishing that which is divinely intended.

NOTES

1. Henry H. Mitchell, *The Recovery of Preaching* (San Francisco: Harper & Row, 1977), 162.

2. P. T. Forsyth, *Positive Preaching and the Modern Mind* (Grand Rapids, Mich.: Eerdmans, 1964), 15.

3. Robert J. Karris, *Luke: Artist and Theologian* (New York: Paulist Press, 1990), 8.

CHAPTER 5

THE SOLITARY PLACE

Nathan Dell

...and they found him and said to him, "Every one is searching for you."
(Mark 1:37, rsv)

One sabbath day, Jesus was invited to make a pastoral call after worship in the synagogue was over. And he did. He went home with Simon Peter, whose mother-in-law was confined to bed with a severe fever. Jesus went to her bedside, took her by the hand, and sent that fever scampering back from where it came. The woman got up out of bed immediately, in the fullness of her health and physical strength, completely cured.

Well, it did not take long for word to get around. It never does when an anointed preacher is in town. It never does when a preacher shows up with words of grace and truth upon his or her lips. It never does when the healing of souls and bodies constitutes the activities of the preacher ... people hear about it!

So, word of the healing of Peter's mother-in-law spread like wildfire through Capernaum. It was probably about 1 P.M. when Jesus healed Peter's mother-in-law. By 3:30 P.M. the crowd had grown so that one could not even get up to the yard. Many of them were longing for their disabilities to be healed by the wondrous power of Jesus. And Jesus did not disappoint their expectations. From sunset on, perhaps long into the night, Jesus touched fevered bodies with his hands, spoke to tormented minds with his words, and counseled troubled hearts with his wisdom. Individuals who had gone to that house with diseased bodies left there with healthy bodies. Those who had gone there with troubling worries left singing "I've got peace like a river." Some, who had arrived lame and limping, left Jesus walking and leaping. Mark said of Jesus,

63

he healed many that evening. Finally the people went home. The Lord and the members of Peter's household retired to their beds.

Then sometime in the wee hours of the morning, when the first winds of daybreak began rounding up the night shadows and herding the darkness back to its place, Jesus got up and quietly left the house. Mark recorded it this way: "And in the morning, a great while before day, he rose and went out to a lonely place, and there he prayed" (Mark 1:35, RSV).

Meanwhile back at Peter's home, perhaps around breakfast time, the disciples discovered that Jesus had gone. He was not in the house. Simon Peter knew he had to be found. It may be that the crowds who had been to the house the previous night were returning. So Simon led several of the disciples to look for Jesus. "And Simon and those who were with him pursued him, and they found him and said to him, 'Every one is searching for you' " (Mark 1:37, RSV).

One of the commentaries suggested that there was a note of reproach or rebuke in the verb phrase "Every one is searching for you."[1] The word implied some annoyance on the part of the disciples. Apparently, as far as these men were concerned, Jesus was acting carelessly. He was failing to capitalize on the opportunity afforded him by his popularity with the people. Can't you hear the note of reproach in their statement "Every one is searching for you"? "What are you doing here, Jesus?" they asked him. "You should be back at the house. You should be in the midst of all those people who are clamoring for you! Lord, the way you healed so many people yesterday has made you very popular in this town. You ought to take advantage of it. Leave this place and go back to the house right now. Every one is searching for you."

May I suggest to those who preach and minister the Word that you be on guard for these words Peter addressed to Jesus: "Every one is searching for you." Let me explain. Jesus was out there alone, hidden away in seclusion. But in fact, he was further preparing himself for his ministry and mission into Galilee. He apparently made preparation for ministry a priority. In this instance, prayer was the particular activity of preparation; preparation carried out in solitude. Matthew Henry was right: "Those that have

isolation

the most business in public, and of the best kind, must sometimes be alone with God; must retire into solitude, there to converse with God and keep communion with him."[2] Jesus had "come to the garden alone." He was looking toward the hills from whence his help comes. Jesus was seeking the strength and insight that only communion and fellowship with God provide. That prayer preparation was an indispensable necessity to having blessing in his words, healing in his touch, vision in his eyes, and strength in his ministry.

So when Peter and the other three disciples broke in on Jesus early that morning, it was his period of preparation they sought to interrupt. It was this activity of preparation they invited him to abandon when they told him "every one is searching for you."

My brothers and sisters in the ministry, as it was with Jesus, so should it be with us. Preparation is an indispensable necessity for those who answer Christ's call to preach the gospel. Of course we need the preparation of prayer. But preachers and pastors also need the preparation of disciplined study. Those preachers who attend seminary need the preparation of classroom and textbook. But all preachers need the preparation of mental inquiry and spiritual investigation of the teachings in the Holy Book. Recall the advice Paul gave to young Timothy with regards to the preparation of study: "Study to show thyself approved of God; a workman who need not be ashamed, rightly dividing the word" (2 Timothy 2:15, KJV, paraphrased). Recall also the request Paul made in his own behalf when he learned that Timothy was coming to visit him in his prison cell at Rome: "When you come, bring the cloak that I left with Carpus at Troas, also the books" (2 Timothy 4:13, RSV). This inspired apostle, who was to write a large part of the New Testament, felt the need to study the words and thoughts that others had written.

In the course of your ministry you will need to study. You will of necessity withdraw from the congregation, from the officers of the church, from your community, to a solitary place called a study. That study may be a library, a church office, or a little room and a table somewhere in your house. Whatever the nature of your study, there you will engage yourself in the activity of preparation.

For preaching and teaching require wisdom and understanding. Preaching and teaching require exposure to the Holy Word and the literature examining that Word. Preaching and ministry demand hard mental labor, prayer, and an endless searching of the deep things of God, revealed in the Scriptures. So preachers will want to form Jesus' habit of arising and making your way to a solitary place. You may or may not get in your study a "good while before day," but whatever the time, make your way there; wherever the location, make your way there. Whatever the size of your study, be it a large office or a kitchen table, make your way there — where your books, Bibles, commentaries, and other resources are. Every preacher needs a solitary place, a place apart from other activities, a place apart from other duties. You need a location to which the preacher or teacher may withdraw for thought and reflection; where you may withdraw to engage your mind and soul in the preparation of study. This is the first observation I discern in this text.

As I take a second look at the text, I see another suggestion, another observation concerning the solitary place. It is this: When you withdraw to your solitary place on a regular basis, when you withdraw to the solitary place daily, at regular hours, there will be those who will pursue you as Peter and those several disciples pursued Jesus. They may be officers of the church who may not understand that there is a relationship between faithful preaching and diligent study. They may be members of the church who may not understand that there is a relationship between standing before the people to deliver the message and spending time before God in a study to receive the message. They will pursue you, Preacher. They may be people from the community who may not understand the difference between all the activities they want you to engage in and the major activity God called you to do: Preach the Word! "Go preach my gospel," says the Lord.

Look at the text. "And Simon and those who were with him followed him, and they found him." Somebody will track the preacher-pastor down. And when they find you, they will want to know "What are you doing here? Every one is looking for you." Some of them will say to you, "As good as you can already preach, what are you doing spending so much time and energy studying?

As well as you know the Good Book, what are you doing in a library, pondering all those other books? What are you doing listening to some mentor or teacher, when Christ promised that the Holy Spirit would teach you and 'lead you into all truth'? With all that going for you, what are you doing expending so much of your time, effort, and preparation in a study?"

There are persons, and some of them may be colleagues, who seek to pull you away from preparation. They will engage you in numerous other activities: entertainment, social functions, community projects, and the like. They will have you rendering service at this post and that; making large commitments of yourself to this organization and that organization. "Everyone is searching for you, Preacher."

And if the preacher is popular, people will seek you out for these activities all the more. This is not to say pastors, preachers, and church professionals are to refrain from participating in the economic, political, and social life of the community. Neither is it to say that we are not to give any leadership in these areas. Rather it is to counsel us not to neglect adequate preparation for preaching and ministry. It is to counsel us not to forget the importance of the "solitary place."

Yes, many people will be searching for you. When they find you in your study spending time in preparation for ministry, they will ask, "What are you doing here?" Sisters and brothers, if you are blessed with good social skills and organizational abilities, if the Lord has provided you with a creative mind and fluency with words, the temptation to forsake the solitary place of preparation will be all the more enticing. Even if we consider ourselves to be full of the Holy Spirit and to possess great spiritual depths, we may be tempted to ignore the solitary place of study.

Preachers who are serving pastorates now, or who will do so at some later date, do well to give appropriate attention to the solitary place of preparation. We do well to give due regard to the study and to the preparation of our heart and soul. We do well to give sufficient attention to the preparation of our mind and message. The preacher ought to be among those who give high value to the solitary place.

And if we need a model by which to see how it is done, we have an excellent example in the Christ. He is the model for making use of the solitary place. On the occasion of this text and on other occasions when people tried to entice him away from his solitary place, Jesus refused to be drawn away from those periods of private spiritual preparation. He did not abandon those periods of soul preparation. And all the Gospels make it so clear that the experience of preparation paid rich dividends. For when Jesus returned from the solitary place, he always did so renewed in strength and power. Luke sums it up well: "And Jesus returned in the power of the Spirit into Galilee" (Luke 4:14, RSV). This is why when he preached and taught, those who heard him reported that "he taught as one who had authority, and not as the scribes" (Mark 1:22, RSV). I think Jesus had been in the solitary place. Mark reported that the people "were astonished at his teaching" (1:22, RSV).

One day a Roman officer sent soldiers to arrest Jesus and bring him in. But the soldiers returned without Jesus. The commanding officer asked them why hadn't they arrested Jesus as they were ordered to do. The soldier's reply went something like this: "Sir, if you had heard him teach as we did, you probably would not have arrested him. If you had heard the power in his voice and the authority in his words as we did, we doubt that you would have arrested him; for 'no man ever spoke like this man' " (John 7:46, RSV). I think Jesus had been readied by his use of the solitary place. So he could speak in the power of the Spirit. He could preach in the power of the Spirit. He could do ministry in the power of the Spirit. And he is our model.

And as preachers and teachers of the church follow Jesus' example at this point, we become better proclaimers of the Word. As preachers and teachers of the church frequent the solitary place of study, we become better heralds of the Good News. For when we frequent the solitary place, Christ enables us to go in and out among our people "in the power of the Spirit." As we keep our appointment with the solitary place, Christ empowers us to do ministry "in the power of the Spirit."

So let preachers dare frequent some solitary place of preparation, and God will sanctify to us that place of study. God will sanctify to us the activity of holy reflection. Then when the man or woman stands to proclaim the gospel, we won't have to rely on borrowed authority alone; that is, we won't have to rely alone upon that authority that comes from merely quoting what others have said. For in the solitary place, God gives preachers and teachers the authority of divine insight. God enables us to think God's thoughts after him. In the solitary place, Christ gives us "the authority of personal conviction," conviction that grows out of personal communion with truths and insights we gathered from the solitary place of preparation.

Brothers and sisters who continue in the ongoing preparation for ministry and mission, this word from the Gospel of Mark challenges us to tarry in the solitary place. Tarry there with our Bible and tools of preparation. Tarry with interest and inquiry. Tarry in daily devotion. Tarry with petition and preparation. And Jesus Christ will see to it that instead of our preaching being clothed in beautiful illustrations and lovely figures of speech, our speech will proceed from our mouths "in demonstration of the Spirit and of power" (1 Corinthians 2:4, RSV).

It may seem troublesome to spend a lot of time, effort, and energy in the solitary place of preparation. It may seem to be a waste of opportunities we would have for other activities. But we will discover it to be just the opposite. For when the Master uses our preaching to be a blessing to the faith community, we will appreciate the solitary place. For as we go there, Christ makes our preaching an effective word to warn the idle and to encourage the fainthearted. Frequent the solitary place; Christ fashions our teaching into a word that will support the weak, teach those who have never heard the message of salvation. As we frequent the solitary place, Christ empowers our message to reclaim the lost and to bring the prodigal back home. In the solitary place Christ gives our preaching the power to rejoice the saints.

"And in the morning, a great while before day, he rose and went out to a solitary place." Let us praise God for the privilege of the solitary place. Let us thank God for the hidden springs of authority flowing to us from the solitary place. Let us bless God's name for the secret source of power God confers upon us in the solitary place. Let us thank God for every vision granted us there, for every anointing poured upon us there, for every word of truth disclosed to us there. The name of the Lord be praised for his gift of the solitary place!

Notes

1. William L. Lane, *The Gospel According to Mark* (NICNT; Grand Rapids, Mich.: Eerdmans, 1974), 82.

2. Matthew Henry, *Matthew Henry's Commentary* (Grand Rapids, Mich.: Zondervan Publishing House, 1961), 1366.

CHAPTER 6

THE MORAL TASK OF AFRICAN AMERICAN PREACHING

Samuel Kelton Roberts

> The Black Church and pulpit must, at whatever cost, have both personal integrity and Black relevance.
> —Henry H. Mitchell, *Black Preaching*

African American preaching has long been hailed as an exemplar of rhetorical brilliance, oratorical fervor, and affective power. Moreover, the tradition of preaching among black people in America has long been associated with the enterprise of challenging unjust social orders and the ability to utter words with such power and determination that social change occurred. When the black preacher spoke, things changed. The prophetic tradition within black preaching has resonated the righteous indignation of Old Testament prophecy. The black preacher, like the Old Testament prophets, called an unjust nation to repentance and righteousness. From Nat Turner, through Adam Clayton Powell Jr., culminating in the person of Martin Luther King Jr., black preaching has stirred a people and prodded a nation to move, however haltingly, toward social righteousness. And, to be sure, the African American preacher has been recognized as the moral exemplar within the believing community, the one regarded and held up as a paragon of moral virtues.

Commentators and scholars have long noted the various functions of preaching: to personify the proclamation of God's Word; to assure believers of the presence and grace of God; to exhort hearers toward a decision to follow Christ and assume a life of discipleship. Somewhat less recognized, however, has been the moral task of preaching itself, particularly the moral task of the preaching moment in the African American pulpit. A guiding presumption of this chapter is that, aside from the power and person of the preacher, the act of preaching itself has elements that are amenable to ethical analysis.

On the surface, there does not seem to be an overt ethical role of preaching outlined in Henry Mitchell's first book on preaching, the ground-breaking *Black Preaching*. Aside from treating the black sermon as a genre worthy of serious scholarship, in that book Mitchell also seemed intent on making the black sermon relevant to the black struggle for liberation. We must remember that the book was written during the height of the renaissance of black theological consciousness. One of the goals of the book seemed to call the black preacher accountable to the task of making sermons relevant to the hardscrabble life most black people faced in the urban ghettos of America. At the same time, the sermon was hailed as the preacher's task of celebrating God's beneficent presence in the lives of black people. While the book was not concerned with discerning the ethical dimension of the black sermon, an implied ethical concern was the extent to which the black sermon helped people toward their eventual liberation from racist structures in American life. And, historically, Mitchell found the black sermon wanting. On the one hand, while there was plenty of evidence that the best of black preaching defied the popular stereotype that it was unduly otherworldly, Mitchell could still affirm soberly that "the most ardent Black churchman must concede that the best of Black preaching and worship has tended to be an *end in itself*."[1] Moreover, Mitchell went on to say that for the most part such preaching has tended to heal *individuals* — to celebrate and support black identity and support the church — but not to involve either folk or institution adequately in some scheme for liberation.[2] It is this suggestion by Mitchell that the sermon ought to point beyond itself that seems intriguing thirty years after the publication of *Black Preaching*. This chapter seeks to affirm the thesis that preaching itself has a moral task and that the analysis of this phenomenon within the African American context can offer a unique perspective on the dynamics at work within the preaching moment.

1. You must find the place 'location to com

2. You may not spend a long time " good while before day "

3.

At the outset of this chapter, a distinction must be made between preaching on moral issues and the moral task of preaching itself. The two are not necessarily the same. The former is more easily (and possibly more superficially) done. In this regard, all the preacher need do is to perform adequate research on a moral issue, find a suitable text to justify the assertions made in the sermon, and then muster a sufficient level of righteous indignation or passion during the delivery of the sermon. With the latter, however, the moral task of preaching, the concern is not so much to preach about that which is moral as to seek the level at which the preaching moment itself becomes a moral act. I hold that there is a moral task inherent in preaching itself. the moral task of preaching

When we speak of the morality of anything, we have in mind a judgment relative to its relative identity with that which we have judged to be good or praiseworthy. When we judge something or someone to be morally good or defensible, our judgment must, of course, find justification in what we call warrants or foundations for our statements. In Christian ethics, the sources for notions of the good can range from the normative authority discerned in Scripture, tradition, human reason, or even some ideological ideal, an example of which would be, say, the presumption of universal equality of men and women. At any rate, we must ground our assertions as to what is good in a standard other than our own views. Otherwise, ethical reflection would devolve to the unfortunate level of personal arguments about personal views about what is good.

Aristotle taught that all human action is oriented toward some end or purpose, a *telos*. Perhaps a good starting point in our quest to discern the moral task of black preaching would be to ask what is it that the preacher hopes to achieve in a sermon. What is her intent or purpose with regard to the listener? If any behavioral change is intended within the listener, what kind of change does he have in mind? What values inform the desired change as opposed to another kind of change? Of course, in back of this question is a prior consideration of what exactly is a sermon. Only when we adequately define what a sermon is can we then be in a position to judge what a good sermon does. So, if Aristotle is correct, then our judgment of the goodness of a sermon must be based on what we determine that a sermon must do. We are drawn inexorably back to the question of the *telos* of the sermon, its end or purpose. This chapter affirms that a sermon in the African American social context has an ethical purpose; it has a moral task.

A sermon might be defined as a human discourse on a divinely inspired truth, proclaimed for the purpose of eliciting within a hearer profound wonder about God, an assurance of God's intent for the human condition, and a quickened desire to live according to divinely inspired precepts. For the purposes of ethical analysis, this chapter proceeds on the assumption that in the preaching moment at least three critical elements are involved. They are a person (A), preaching to person (B), for the purpose of eliciting (in B) a certain desired ethical state (C). All three of these elements are related and can never really be separated one from the other. Within the total context of the preaching moment, they have no meaning apart from the other two. A sermon can never be merely a personal meditation thought in silence or a soliloquy uttered in privacy; it must be spoken and directed toward an *other* person. To this extent, the sermon is always a social event, communicated and proclaimed within the social bonds of a community of believers. This raises the interesting possibility that while the sermon presumes the reality of God, it is not so much directed to God as to those hearers who themselves believe in God. If directed to God only and not to the hearers, the sermon would have a vastly different outcome and purpose; it would be a personal meditation. If, however, the sermon is directed to another human person, then that sermon must in some fundamental way communicate with that person at the deepest level possible if the sermon's intent is to be fulfilled.

Thus the sermon presumes a critical interaction or relationship between the one from whom the sermon comes and the one to whom the sermon is directed. We must presume that the sermon is preached to and is received by each individual in the audience or congregation. Thus the presumption that the sermon is wholly directed to the congregation is false and somewhat shallow; that assertion is only part of the phenomenon of the preaching moment.

Persons make up congregations. Fred B. Craddock is so cognizant of this fact that he urges readers of *Preaching* to "let the names of the listeners come to mind and be formed by the lips."[3] Each person listens to the sermon with his or her own presuppositions, background, personal problems and issues in mind as they listen to the sermon on that occasion. Thus at some critical level there is a powerful connection between the person offering the sermon and the person hearing and receiving the sermon.

At this point, we may hazard a thesis relative to the moral task of preaching. The moral task of preaching is to quicken a hearer's will to seek and follow God. As the preacher leads the hearer in contemplating a profound wonder about God and God's grace extended, the will of the hearer is sharpened and made more resolute to live fully for God.

At this point the question comes as to what necessary conditions must be met in order for the preacher to be in critical contact with the hearer such that the intended ethical result comes to pass. What must A (preacher) do or embody in order that B (hearer) can remain in a relationship such that C (ethical goal) is achieved?

There are at least two levels on which the interaction between the preacher and hearer can proceed. At one level, there is the realm of the cognitive. At this level the interaction between the two is primarily in the realm of ideas, concepts, and beliefs that are known and understandable to the hearer. At this level the minds of two persons are in relationship; one mind must be understood by another for the sermon to have some level of coherence and meaning. Can the focus on the purely cognitive lead to the desired ethical state as envisioned in our thesis? It is doubtful. We may therefore discount the purely cognitive as the basis on which our hope for ethical transformation is to take place, for a will to be quickened to follow and live fully for God.

There is another level of interaction, and this is at the level of the purely affective, the level of the emotional. Can the preacher exude a sufficient degree of personal warmth and charisma such that our desired ethical change can come about? While it is possible that an ethical transformation might be brought about as a result of the heat of passion symptomatic of the emotional sermon, it is also possible that the resolve to remain in such a state will dissipate over a period of time. Clearly, more is needed. It is only through a deeper analysis of the will of the hearer, that aspect of the hearer's makeup that involves both the cognitive and the affective, that we shall gain some insight into how the ethical goal of preaching might be reached.

No act intended by a human being comes to pass unless that act is forged by the human will. Moreover, that which human beings intend to bring to pass is initially an idea that is brought into reality by human desire. Thus all intentioned human acts must involve the cognitive and affective realms of human nature. Unless we desire an idea to come to reality it remains dormant; it remains only an idea. Human will is therefore the powerful union of the affective and cognitive aspects of our nature. Human will is the harnessing of affective desire for the embodiment of an idea. Vision achieved through cognition awaits the power of desire in order for an act to be completed. With respect to achieving our ultimate goal in the preaching task of quickening the will of the hearer, we may presume that if this goal is to be met then the preacher must relate to the hearer at both the cognitive and the affective levels. For it is only at these levels that the will of the hearer can be engaged and subsequently quickened.

Continuing our focus on the hearer, we may presume that the hearer of a sermon has already acted upon his or her will to even be in the physical context to hear a sermon. Each listener, by virtue of his or her presence in the preaching moment, declares either curiosity about that which is expected to be declared or tacit approval of that which is expected to be declared. Either way, the person present has already indicated and acted upon his or her will to be there. But clearly, more is desired: perhaps a desire to have a continuing hunger about a clearer disclosure of God's presence; perhaps the need to secure a greater level of inspiration, perhaps insight into how to approach an impending problem or issue. Resolution of these latter issues is what the listener desires and needs. Or it may be that what listeners really desire is an internal transformation such that they will be able to meet any type of situation. After all, it is highly unlikely that a preacher will be preaching on the specific issue that a person is directly interested in. Thus it is personal transformation that must be the burden of the ethical task of the preacher or the preaching moment, and it is the personal transformation that the hearer seeks.

Henry Mitchell points us to this moment when he discusses the final phase of the black sermon, the so-called celebration. At this point in the sermon, there is a shift from the "objective fact to subjective testimony — from 'he said' and 'it happened' to 'I feel' and 'I believe.' "[4] This is precisely the fusion of the cognitive and the affective realms of human nature. All that has preceded the celebration has invited cognitive assent from the hearer. The moment of celebration, however, elicits affective desire to fulfill and embody the cognitive vision outlined earlier by the preacher. The integrity of the sermon, for Mitchell, is assured only when the affective dimension seeks to embody a fully developed cognitive vision. Thus, in African American parlance, a sermon "with all gravy and no meat" is inauthentic. It is structurally inadequate from a purely technical point of view and morally bankrupt from an ethical point of view. From such a posture, Mitchell could admonish an entire generation of black preachers to prepare for sermons lest they violate this union between the cognitive and the affective. Says Mitchell, "there must be some serious effort to give God one's best in preparation."[5] Moreover, the "celebration should not obscure the need to make the sermon relevant to the real life concerns of people." As Mitchell says, "the sermon which celebrates without giving help is an opiate."[6] Put positively, the ideal sermon in the African American setting would combine "ecstasy and involvement."[7]

The preacher bears a great responsibility in ensuring a relationship with the hearer so that the ethical goal of quickening the will of the latter can be achieved. What is the nature of this relationship? There must be a relationship of trust between hearer and preacher such that the former believes that the latter is worthy enough to be listened to. This would imply that A would possess sufficient knowledge (cognitive), personal warmth (affective), and credibility (moral — I believe in you because you are worthy, which is based on a value judgment). Listeners do not enter into the

dialogical space that is the preaching moment only to gain information (cognitive) or necessarily to gain emotional warmth from
the person doing the preaching (affective). They stay and listen because they believe in the message being proclaimed and also have
a need to believe in the person doing the proclaiming. In *Preaching
for Today*, Clyde E. Fant asserted that credibility was "the weight
given to the assertions of a speaker and the acceptance accorded
them by his hearers. It is composed of two factors, trustworthiness and expertness."[8] The level of expertness on the part of the
preacher desired by the listener is not exclusively mastery of the
factual data referenced in a sermon, although competent appropriation of data does reinforce the listener's desire to grant credibility
to the preacher while incompetent and fraudulent appropriation
of data will tend to distract from credibility. But this is only one
aspect of the data sought by listeners to a sermon. As Fant goes
on to suggest, what the listeners desire in terms of expertness is
some evidence that the person has entered into relationship with
the people. This is how Fant explains it:

> *Expertness* means that as a human being, living among these people in
> this time and in this place, I must know something. I must understand
> the culture in which I live and the living needs of the people to whom I
> minister; and I must know how to interpret the word of God which speaks
> to them. This is my "expertness" as a preacher of the gospel.[9]

In a similar vein, Mitchell asserts that: "In the Black preaching
enterprise, the preacher's preparation starts with close identity
with his congregation. Historically, being Black, he could not es-
cape having a part in their condition even if he wanted to.... The
Black preacher must be up to his ears in the condition of his people,
and out of this comes the easy dialogue between whose lives are intimately close together — so close together that the themes which
invade the consciousness of the one also invade the other."[10] Thus
the preacher comes to the preaching moment with the responsibility of establishing trustworthiness in the minds of the hearers.
Such trustworthiness has a cognitive and an affective aspect, each
related to trustworthiness. A preacher who violates the cognitive
aspect of trustworthiness by affirming a biblical or theological
principle that the hearer knows not to be true will not gain the

trust of the hearer. Similarly, the preacher who cannot or will not share the existential condition with the hearer fares no better. No hearer can trust a preacher if he feels an affective alienation with that preacher. As if to suggest that the way the preacher finds true authenticity, a means whereby he can establish a good relationship with the audience, Mitchell asserts that the preacher must be perceived as one who resonates the same joy in the Lord as the congregation enjoys. "At its best, however, Black worship must have joy in its highest and purest form. At his best, the Black preacher must be not only a teacher and mobilizer, a father figure and an enabler, but also a celebrant. He must have a little of the joy *himself.*"[11]

Inherent in the question of trustworthiness, so critical in the relationship between hearer and preacher, is the matter of personal lifestyle of the preacher. She must be viewed and perceived as one above reproach, a seeker for moral uprightness. His lifestyle should defy the popular but erroneous stereotype of the black preacher as greedy for money and material possessions. Mitchell is aware of this issue and asserts that

> the value system of the Black preacher must project, now, the *servant* image. The competent servant must be reasonably provided for, but if he insists on extremes and has a life style associated with great wealth, then the youth of the new Black masses will be turned off by the church and pulpit. For them, one's scale of values and commitments speaks first and, often, last.[12]

The matter of personal integrity has implications as well in the rather mundane and routine practice of sermon preparation. Even in the onerous task of grinding out sermon after sermon is the preacher required to be aware of the challenge of maintaining moral uprightness. In fact, it is the challenge of preparing sermons, Sunday after Sunday, sometimes more than one, that tempts many preachers to cut corners and produce less than their best. One questionable practice Mitchell warned against that has ethical connotations also goes to the issue of authenticity in sermon preparation: the habit of using canned sermons to mitigate increasingly busy schedules, made for the "man who has to say something rather than the man who has something to say."[13] The preaching moment always bears with it the challenge to issue a fresh word from the Lord to hearers who crave spiritual replenishment.

Finally, if the preacher has been found trustworthy enough by the hearers so that their wills are transformed during the preaching moment, then we would expect our ethical goal of quickening a desire to live fully for God to have been accomplished. Moreover, if the quickening is of sufficient depth, then at least two needless burdens are spared the preacher. One, the preacher is spared the dubious burden of believing that unless she isolates particular and specific ethical issues as the central core of the sermon, a moral task has not been accomplished. Implicit in this mistaken belief is the feeling that a sermon is a failure, ethically speaking, if it has not spoken out on a particular issue. Our thesis would suggest that all sermons have an ethical task, and that task is to quicken the will of the hearer so that he becomes disposed to live fully according to the will of God. This disposition to live fully according to God's will goes far deeper than being sensitive to particular and discrete ethical issues, although such sensitivity is bound to ensue within the consciousness of persons who live within the will of God. Second, the preacher need not feel obliged to regard the sermon as a failure, ethically speaking, if the members of a congregational audience are not all moved to storm the barricades relative to some particular and specific ethical issue immediately after the sermon. The quiet storm within that is stirred when the will becomes quickened to live fully for God is all that is required at the preaching moment. Such quickening will inevitably move the people of God to action against injustice or any ethical ill that is contrary to the will of God. Such action comes, however, out of a changed disposition within these persons rather than the result of momentary excitement about one particular ethical issue. Thus, while hearers might be motivated in a sermon to feel outrage, for example, against a specific case of police brutality, the truly transformed souls will be outraged against human brutality everywhere, in all contexts, and under all conditions. And, they will let the local precinct captain know of their outrage ultimately, but such outrage has grown out of will that has now become disposed to fight brutality everywhere. The preaching moment has touched a level of ethical sensitivity that goes deep; it seeks a type of moral discernment and readiness for action that is sensitive to the fact that God is against brutality and injustice everywhere, unfairness in all contexts of human living.

Thus, preaching, to the extent that it always has a moral task, is spared from the rather superficial approach of feeling that a sermon has not fulfilled its ethical task unless it has addressed a specific moral or social problem. Enticing the will to become sharpened to follow the will of God is the task of the sermon. And a hearer need not be disappointed if a sermon does not spell out specific details relative to ethical issues personally important to that believer, for whenever a preacher makes known God's grace meted out unstintingly to all, then such grace made available to that hearer will be perceived. Such a hearer is bound, as well, to be motivated to live for God out of gratitude. The ethical end of the preaching moment has been achieved. Preaching has fulfilled its moral task.

NOTES

1. Henry H. Mitchell, *Black Preaching* (New York: Harper & Row, 1979), 214, emphasis added.

2. Ibid.

3. Fred B. Craddock, *Preaching* (Nashville: Abingdon, 1985), 92.

4. Mitchell, 188–89.

5. Ibid., 198.

6. Ibid., 209.

7. Ibid., 216.

8. Clyde E. Fant, *Preaching for Today* (New York: Harper & Row, 1975), 68.

9. Ibid., 69.

10. Mitchell, 103–4.

11. Ibid., 210.

12. Ibid., 225.

13. Ibid., 226.

CHAPTER 7

OF SELF, SOUND, AND SACREDNESS

VICTORIA L. PRATT

This essay seeks to honor Henry Mitchell for his ground-breaking efforts in the work of reclaiming the cultural and spiritual roots of an African religious past. Indeed, the works of Henry and Ella Mitchell have been instrumental in repositioning African belief and religious philosophy to their rightful place within the context of African American religious life and expression.[1]

Cultures everywhere naturally embrace particular ways of explaining their existence and interpreting their relationship to the cosmos. What is little understood and often omitted in the discussion of African American religion, however, is the relationship between the African idea of God and the Christianity that the slaves adopted. In fact, most substantive discussion of African anthropology within the context of Western theology is extremely limited or else very distorted. Central to African religious belief is the idea that God is a supreme being who is the basis for all existence and who creates unity and balance in all life. God's life force is enfolded and revealed throughout the universe. This core belief is fundamental to the cohesiveness and vitality of life and well being of persons and community. It is systematically reinforced through ritual practices in the life of community through sayings, stories, myths, and proverbs, and then is passed on through the generations. Despite the great cultural diversity evident across the continent, as well as the tremendous external influences imposed upon Africa over time, this core belief has remained intact.

The discussion here builds upon Henry Mitchell's work and further contends that dimensions of African spirituality and religious belief systems can be crucial to the development of African American religious consciousness. Further, African beliefs about God can be instrumental in the evolution of a theological method that is responsive to the relationship between peoples of the African Diaspora and European Christian theology. The African American pastor, Christian educator, and layperson are challenged through Mitchell's work to become engaged in the quest for contextual interpretation of the gospel in light of its historical misappropriation by those who sought to diminish the meaning of African belief. Through both calculated effort and ignorance of cultural interpretations about God, there has been a systematic devaluation of African human worth, spiritual wisdom, and personhood. This has had a devastating effect upon the psyche of peoples of African descent. The institution of slavery and the experience of colonization engendered a mode of Christianity that was intentionally used to recondition thinking, modify behavior, and control the lives of the slave. This has been well documented.[2] It follows that the challenge of correcting the violations to people, of history, and to the gospel truth rests in the realm of theological concern.

A summary of the questions raised in Mitchell's book and discussed in this chapter are as follows: What is the relevance of African belief within contemporary African American life and religious concern? How might insight about God and community be intentionally woven into the fabric of African American religious expression, corporate worship, and Christian education as a corrective to conventional Western dogmatics and cultural bias? How might theological method be developed that affirms the fullness of a people's experience with God, brings validation to those historically cast aside, as well as reconciliation of both oppressor and victim back to the design of God's purpose and creation? What is further suggested here is that the African American preacher, Christian educator, and theologian play crucial roles and bear a particular responsibility toward the development of enlightened and relevant hermeneutical processes.

The book *Black Belief* was first published in 1975, a quarter of a century ago, at a time of heightened interest and activity in African history and culture. African studies programs, black theology, liberation theology, increased Africentric emphasis within seminary and academic life are the result of this period of intense research into our African past. But even as we enter a new millennium, and after twenty-five event-filled years of scholarship, we do not seem any closer to reappropriating this enormous body of healing wisdom nor appreciating its potential function in the revitalization of people and community. While reference to African belief systems may now be more acceptable, they are rarely included as a part of mainstream theological investigation, biblical study, or worship life. We feel free to dress up African in our churches, hold African festivals, adopt African names, search for validation of African presence in biblical history. Rarely, however, is the activity directed toward a more holistic appreciation, appropriation, and celebration of the voice of God as it actively speaks to a people through history and ancestors, in a divine continuum of space and time.

The African understanding of God, which will be referred to in this chapter as African belief, cannot be so easily dismissed. Deeper exploration reveals that it is born of a people of the beginning who thrived in the cradle of time between the Tigris and Euphrates rivers; a people whose being reflected the image of God from the primal waters of creation; who recorded their connection to God and their attunement with creation right from the beginning in ancient stories and song, dance and music for thousands of years. Through the voice and urgings of the ancestors throughout the African Diaspora, we can discern the echo of words of wisdom, inspiration, and teachings that foster the wholesome development of persons and community. A deeper appreciation of African belief can help to provide a sense of purpose, continuity, and reconnection to people and times past. Through the conscientious unraveling of distorted perceptions about African belief in the past, we may now attend to the festering wounds of generations present. This chapter can only explore the meaning of God in African belief conceptually because the body of knowledge is far too extensive to elaborate here.[3] The reader is invited to embark upon his or her own personal journey of discovery and thus begin to midwife the spiritual births of new generations of African American Christians, newly empowered with a clearer sense of belonging and appreciation for that which God continues to brings to us through Christ. For in his transcendent, inclusive presence,

Christ is assigned neither gender, economic status, nor national identity. The challenge offered to us here is not unlike that of the early Christians who, like Paul, a Jew turned Christian, ministers to Gentiles, and systematically builds upon cultural insights that communicate the fullness of the gospel message.[4]

RENEWING THE MIND

> Be not conformed to this world: but be ye transformed by the renewing of your mind. (Romans 12:2, KJV)

The fundamental, ontological dynamic of African belief is God. God lives in and through all creation and is the vital force who makes being possible and who assigns the responsibility of caring for creation to humans.[5] The ancestors are only a prayer away and hold constant vigil over the well-being of community. This primal relationship with God, whose beingness permeates everything, is at the core of black belief that followed the children of the Diaspora wherever they were carried. Christ, to the enslaved African, became the personal manifestation of God's life force. He became intimately involved in the business of survival of those fragmented peoples broken off from the whole and disconnected from the homeland. This was well depicted in the movie *Amistad* by the main character, Cinque. As he attempted to tell the story of his capture into slavery, he bent over, picked up a stick, and drew a line on the ground to indicate how far he had come across the ocean. Then later, we saw how another slave recognized the special power of the Christ when he was shown Bible illustrations of Jesus performing healing miracles. Christ met the enslaved African in the throes of crisis, and this Christ engendered the belief that they had not been forgotten or abandoned. Christ seemed to be the impetus for renewed hope that the dynamic force of God is unfailing. The foundational layer of faith for African Christians in America was set into motion through the personal saving actions of God made real in the presence of Christ.

While the religious beliefs of every society define expectations, evaluations, and judgments deemed important for self-understanding and standards of morality, the provisions for such are by no means the same everywhere. European settlers in the New World entered as strangers in a strange land themselves, trying to make sense of the environment, create new possibilities and relationships with God, and relate to the native peoples and land. But rather than effect a new way of relating through religion and social interaction, they managed to repeat old patterns and relationships acquired in the Old World. The religion of the Middle Ages into which the African was enslaved had no place for the dynamism of God as seen through African imagination. Attempts were systematically made to dissect this long memory from the minds of the African, but it persisted deep in the hearts of the people. Considered subhumans, Africans were not even given credit for their profound experience with and knowledge about God.[6]

In contrast to African belief, the God of European imagination was perceived to exist outside the realm of daily human experience. The Western interpretation of God resulted in the creation of divisions between human and divine, boundaries between clergy and laity, ruler and peasant, Indian and white settler, African and European, good and evil, the sacred and profane. From the moment of conception, humanity began its process of devolution, struggling in a life long battle between spirit and flesh, in a progressive, downward movement from divine realms to damnation and darkness. From Augustine to the Western Christianity of Renaissance Europe, the desire to achieve intimacy with God was thwarted by negative perceptions and definitions of self, by the persistent shadow of original sin and the weakness of human flesh. The human spirit seemed inevitably condemned to an existence of suffering, always falling short of God's grace. The glory of God was viewed through this shattered prism that reflected the painfully broken fragments of self and the entire creation.[7]

In every culture, children quickly learn to respond to the assessments of society that are transmitted by parents, elders, and kin. Beliefs about who we are, where we come from, our purpose for living are all part of the religious impulse to link human to Creator, to provide relevant definitions of self and a sense of belonging. Beliefs shape our attitudes, inform behavior, nurture vision, and drive a people to personal or collective action in the process of survival. But despite the life-negating spiritual directives and life-threatening controls exerted over the African, the dynamism of African belief continued to thrive. It set the stage for Christian belief that would eventually foster the creation of Spiritual music and motivate a people to survive. What men intended for evil was, in faith, turned into good through the reimaged reality of the Christ.[8]

The charge to African Americans within the text quoted above compels us to the work of spiritual renewal of mind with the same creative drive as that of our ancestors. Renewal means making new *again*. The mind of African American Christians and African Diaspora Christians has been so conditioned by a diminished sense of self, so indoctrinated with contradictory Christian doctrine, that there is a serious challenge and loud call for renewed definitions of self and for personal transformation. The diminished perceptions of self, thoroughly internalized during our fragmented experience in the New World, are in need of being made whole again. Following the principles of Christ and the path that leads toward transformation will be problematic as long as conventional doctrine remains skewed with the theological contradictions, distortions, and cultural biases of Old World Christian belief.

For African American Christians, renewing the mind is a process that I suggest must include confronting and getting rid of the diminished sense of self that was reinforced during our history of bondage; eliminating from our minds the image of self and disabling beliefs we have acquired in a fundamentally racist society; reconnecting to the healing insights about God communicated through African belief; returning to the ground of all being, knowledge, and possibility, whom we identify as our supreme creator God; reacquainting ourselves with the proverbs and stories of African belief that reconnect us to the God of all time, to one another, and to community; surrendering our lives to the awakening spirit of the living God within, whom we experience as the Christ; committing to the realization and activation of the Christ within, through actions in the world as persons of new being possibility: thinking, doing, and experiencing life in a profoundly different way. Freed from the bondage of dysfunctional belief and negative conditioning, we can then be released to the possibility of transformation and be liberated to enjoy the responsibility of a mind truly renewed in Christ. The model outlined above is, I believe, in keeping with what Theophus Smith refers to as "pharmacopeic praxis" in *Conjuring Culture*.[9] This is a form of "theological homeopathy" that utilizes beliefs once perceived by the slave holder as being poisonous but now intentionally reappropriated for the purposes of healing and empowerment. "Toxic forces" once used to victimize a people can become curative when reassessed and reenvisioned toward the creative designs of God. It is certainly possible for African belief to be reassessed with these healing perspectives and holy objectives in mind.

Renewal of the mind must also include an intentional process for the restructuring of thoughts and behavior, work that is an outgrowth of the initial conversion experience and encounter with Christ. Such a process creates a fertile ground and foundation upon which the teachings of Christ are seeded. A model for pharmacopeic praxis was demonstrated for us by our African foreparents. They brought with them an innate understanding of nature, animal husbandry, and agricultural cultivation that slave holders used for their own exploitative purposes. Slaves, however, incorporated their particular cultural experience of God in ways not predictable by their masters. Their understanding of God helped them to adapt with resilience to their new physical world despite the hardships imposed upon them. They "conjured" recreative interpretations of biblical texts and parables that were fundamentally informed by their perceptions of God and nature.[10] Not only were they enabled to reaffirm their experience with the vital force of God within all creation; they also conjured a revolutionary interpretation of a Christ whose seed grows within human consciousness and liberates oppressed peoples. The foundational layering of African belief and implicit connection to the supreme God resulted in a newly grounded Christian belief that was turned against slaveholders. The coded language that was developed within the music of Spirituals is an example of the convergence of African belief within a reimagined Christian context.[11]

Rather than the subduing the human spirit, as was hoped for by the slave holder, the reimaged Christ of the slave reinforced a reconnection to the dynamic presence of God who just shows up, who makes a way out of no way, and incites the mind to throw off the shackles of bondage. Old Testament stories quickened the imagination of slaves, who could easily identify with the tribal experience of the ancient Hebrew people and with their movement into and out of bondage.

While the colonial experience in Africa and the New World may differ in significant ways, Christianity is a major link between them. Both African and African American theologians share similar concerns as we attempt to reexamine and uncover a relevant hermeneutic and community experience that interprets the Christianity adapted by peoples of the African Diaspora. The African scholar C. B. Baeta[12] goes on further to boldly suggest that African history, tradition, spiritual wisdom, and culture are so rich that an African Christian theology may conceivably be developed without exclusively focusing upon Hebrew law, tradition, and religious history. It is not necessary to completely agree with this his suggestion in order to understand his implication that the God of all creation speaks to tribal civilizations across culture and engenders transformation and well being to people throughout time.

African belief presents an amazing contrast to the testimony and perception of God and to the Christian message communicated by European believers. African belief embraces the idea of the universe as a whole and human beings as gift of the creator. Humans are endowed with *muntu*, a dynamic energy or life force that comes from God[13] and moves throughout created life and the cycle of life like seeds toward the sun. Humans evolve and thrive in a gradual process, connected to God, nurtured by kin, learning from elders the sacred wisdom necessary to human growth, productivity, and moral concern. The African, throughout, perceived of the self as being part of the whole complex of created life, valued for creative abilities, contributions to creation and community, and in full possession of a dignity and worth that could never be diminished or discarded, and always possible to be redeemed. Destruction to life or community values could not take place without affecting the whole, and consequences of such destruction could not be treated lightly. The ancestors who came before are always connected to the whole and call to mind biblical encounters with God and ancestors of the Christian faith. Just as teachers of the law of Moses appear in a cloud of witness, God is always present to each generation in African belief. There are always three generations present at the same time: ancestors who are closest to God (the living dead),[14] the present, living generation, and those about to be born. The ancestors remain available, whispering the cautionary, life-sustaining wisdom from God, who makes a way out of no way and who calls the people ever forward in faith and wholeness.

Reviving Through Sound

In the beginning was the Word, and the Word was with God.
(John 1:1, kjv)

Out of the abundance of the heart the mouth speaketh.
(Matthew 12:34, kjv)

African belief engenders a deep appreciation for the regenerative features of sound. The worship experience of African Americans is an extension of that belief and spiritual legacy connected to sound. The particular sense-ability of African people to sound perception is evident in every aspect of religious expression. The rootedness of sound in primal experience and religious expression is, of course, a universal phenomenon.[15] Certainly this was true of the ancient Hebrew mystic in his handling of the Hebrew language and sacred text, the Qabala. To the Jewish mystic, a special name and tone was associated with God and assigned to each letter of the Hebrew alphabet. The tones produced were believed to activate divine energy that in turn activated divine consciousness. Each tone was associated with a particular attribute deemed important to the development of a high attunement and connection to God.[16] While there is no written record documenting the use of sacred sound in African tradition, the chants, songs, musical instruments, devices to facilitate memory, storytelling, and dance all attest to the particular sensibility of the African to sound.

In human experience, particularly for indigenous peoples who live in close relationship to the land and whose survival depends upon the bounty of created life, sound arrests the attention and, in a sense, evokes a state of attention in significant ways. The sound of thunder, the crack of lightning, the gush of wind or beat of rain, the call of birds all have spiritual import in African belief. The beat of a heart, the sounds of labor, the first cry at birth, the rasping sounds of breath uttered in the struggle for life in sickness and at the end of life are all connected to a shared understanding of how the life force of God is made manifest.

Cultural interpretations of this phenomenon vary. The name in African belief for the sound of the spiritual force that becomes activated in the physical world is *Nommo*.[17] *Nommo* is a word concept borrowed from the Bantu languages of West Africa and refers to the creative, driving power that gives life to all of creation. It is experienced throughout nature as the mighty awakener of creative potential always present within creation. *Nommo* is heard in nature, in the sound of the voice, in the beat of the drum that imitates the voice and rhythms of nature. *Nommo* cajoles and mocks, strengthens and heals, changes and transforms. Similar to the understanding in Hebrew language that interprets the word *God* as an action-oriented verb, *nommo's* sole reason for existence is to make things happen and create within the never-ending cycles of life and death and rebirth.

Nommo happens because God's creative impulse seeks expression in all of life and in the breath of those called to affirm and uplift life. *Nommo* is echoed in the voice of the preacher, sons and daughters of thunder, whose divine utterances rhythmically appropriate sound in obedience to God and under the power of God's holy, healing spirit. Through the mind and breath of the preacher, sound captivates the senses, refocuses thought, calls the spirit to a state of alertness not evident before a word was spoken. It is almost as though sound creates a spirit of obedience, enabling the mind to receive some deeper level of communication from the realm of the divine, evoking a state of being or readiness to receive the unction from the Holy Spirit. To the African American Christian, there is wonder-working power simply in hearing of the name of Jesus.

The legacy of *nommo* clearly resounds within the context of the African American worship experience. Mitchell refers to this particular worshipful response in *Celebration and Experience in Preaching*.[18] There is a holistic, life-affirming responsiveness in the presence of God. It is manifested in the call-response patterns, within worship, in the movement-evoking sounds of vocal or instrumental music, in the dance of the believer, and the shout of individual or collective praise. The orality of the African tradition is embodied within the totality of the worship experience: the concert of voice, music, rhythm, story, dance, in response to the preached word and urgings of the Holy Spirit. All play an important part in the holistic awakening process of body, mind, and spirit of the worshiper. This presents a strident contrast to the cerebral orientation of the Western religious practice and to the split-consciousness orientation of Renaissance theology. In the worship experience of children of the African Diaspora, there is a fully *felt* call and response to God and creation within body, mind, and spirit. That response is a resounding Amen! While the preached word is conducted through the instrumentality of the voice and with the authority that comes from biblical word, it cannot be experienced as truth without the gestalt of whole-feeling responses. Deeper appreciation of the holistic dimension of African belief compels us to rethink the ways in which our Spirit-filled responses have been distorted by the conventional Christian church and commercialized by American culture. African belief assists us in the process of reclaiming our particular patterns of preaching, worship, and fellowship with one another. Rather than participate in the commodification of cherished worship forms, we are compelled to honor their uniqueness. We are challenged to shield them from the persistent commercial forces that seek to diminish their meaning and function toward the healing of persons and community.

While Mitchell does not specifically address African belief in *Celebration Preaching*, his entire discourse concerning preaching to the whole person nevertheless reminds us of the alienation that was experienced by Africans when confronted with the passive, reflective, dogmatic preachment and worship during the slave and colonial periods. We can appreciate how difficult it must have been for the slave master to effect a total reconditioning within the spirit of the slave.[19] We can also understand what motivated the African to recreate a worshipful experience more in harmony with African belief and the spiritual needs of the slave community. Once again, the orality of the African worship experience can be shared with that of the Hebrew tradition. The oral nature of storytelling, the colorful depiction of characters within the Old Testament, the lyrical stories of the psalmists, the wisdom sayings and proverbs all played a role in the development of an oral tradition that is linked to the orality of the African belief and practice. To the preached word can be added the stories, sayings, proverbs that speak to the cultural memory of our people and bring new insight to the text.

The characteristic features of preaching and worship in our churches are not fully appreciated and are often simplistically categorized as African American religious folk expression. But when we understand the holistic nature of our worship experience and its function in the healing, reconnecting, and reconciling of people back to God, we are in a much better position to effect changes within self and community of faith. We have already lost important ground. So familiar have these worshipful expressions become that are often portrayed in caricature, stereotyped and commercialized by theater, television, in Hollywood, and taken in jest even in our own portrayal of self. This is the danger for a people so conditioned and dependent upon the definitions of others. There is life-negating danger evident in the acceptance of stereotypical preaching styles, worship, and fellowship that are polished and performed for public consumption. But there is always time to remind ourselves of who we really are.

The African American church, whether it was in the wooded hollows of the slave environment, the rural church of Southern legacy, storefront house of worship, or the sophisticated sanctuary of contemporary urban communities can also be interpreted as the incarnation of *nommo*. The church is reenvisioned as a cosmic womb, reappropriated in the African experience for the purpose of reimagining life qualitatively different from the oppressive reality of the world. Church and renewed life are synonymous. Church becomes the sanctified space where people and community can come together, negotiate the Word of God, personally engage the dormant powers of God within the people, and the corporate body of Christ.

The brilliance of this oral tradition is appreciated anew when we can fully experience the hidden, healing dimensions of African American religious expression. One's personal story of limitation and loss can be renegotiated and reenvisioned. The old is released as the allure of the divine invites the broken in spirit to reenter God's larger story. Inside divine space and time there is "plenty good room." *Nommo*, through the thunder of the preacher's voice and lightning of the spirit, facilitates the cosmic process of change. The worshiper is affected at a cellular level within the body-mind, and the saved can sing "Praise God, I know I been changed." *Nommo* is activated through the vocal responses of choir and congregation, in an ever-widening circle, in the call to life and enhanced meaning. A melodic, rhythmic anointing through the allurement of music and sound compels the lame to walk and dance, the blind to see, and the dumb to give voice and renewed sense-ability. Liturgy, grounded in holistic life-affirming purpose, the power of the spoken word, the powerful prayers and invocation of the holy spirits are all linked together in the sacred work of transformation, metanoia through the healing impulse of God's Word. The work of *nommo* is dynamic, as is the awakening potential within the soul of the saved. Transformation is an ongoing enterprise, a call to freedom, accountability, responsibility, and an experienced sense of new order in one's relationship to God, neighbor, and creation. The Christ who is raised up each Sunday morning by the spirited collective energies of the faithful will follow the people in their bodies and into the world in dire need of resurrection. *Nommo*, activated in the therapeutic processes of pastoral care, incites a depressed people to move from disease to discovery, from chaos to order, from human addictions, to right relationships to God. An African song from the Congo echoes the expectation of new order in one's relationship with God:

> Oh Spirit come, come to help us! Many ills beset us here below.
> But let us continue to pray till the end. Oh Spirit come.[20]

And the Spirit keeps coming to us through the refrain sung in our own spiritual music.... "Every time I feel the Spirit, moving in my heart, I will pray!"

RECOVERING THE SACRED

> For we knew that the whole creation groaneth and travaileth in pain to-
> gether until now. And not only they, but ourselves also, which have the
> firstfruits of the Spirit, even we ourselves groan within ourselves, waiting
> for the adoption, to wit, the redemption of our body.
>
> (Romans 8:22–23, KJV)

> Treat the earth well. It was not given to you by your parents; it was lent
> to you by your children.   (Kenyan proverb)

The incarnation of Christ within Christian witness is made manifest through praxis: the intentional, disciplined care of God's creation and relationships within the community called, and through the practice we believe as true. Yet even the truth about a fundamentally ecological African belief system has terribly distorted throughout history and misperceived by African Americans. The participatory, holistic nature of African belief, grounded in the idea of God in and through all creation, is always directed toward the fullness of health, harmony, vitality, and the sacred within creation. God does not exist apart from creation, creating the world and then relinquishing its control for the exclusive dominion by human beings. The preservation of life and survival of community rest in the faithful, collective responses of a people endowed by God, to work with the supreme Creator of all.

We have much to learn from the deep ecological orientation of our ancestors if we are to recover the sacred within our everyday lives. But it means rethinking all that we do and seeing, hearing, experiencing the dynamic and mysterious presence of God everywhere, and affirming what we understand through our actions of care and restoration. What would happen, for example, if we believed, as our foreparents did, that the air, forests, rain, sun, rivers, and plant life are all part of the sacred whole? Or that when honored, they provide safety, nurturance, and healing to the whole of community? What would happen if we truly believed that pregnancy is a blessing from God, that the children born to us are always gifts from God and that they require the constant care and protection from a community who understands their sacred value? The visible and invisible treasures of God, according to this orientation, have no end because God only knows how to give. What God gives to us, we need to take care of. The notion of scarcity, that food or fruit or game or natural resources would become depleted in precolonial Africa, for example, was unthinkable. The primary concern of tribal elders and spiritual leadership was to work in harmony with the ancestors, to be vigilant of any misappropriation or misuse of creation or of actions that threaten the safety and survival of community. The prophetic role of our contemporary sacred specialists, our pastors and educators, calls us to revisit the deep ecology of our foreparents and employ the power of God's Spirit within us to do the same. We can recover this deep dimension of faith and bring new meaning to our ever-evolving covenant with God and to the salvific work of Christ experienced through us.

While praise and praxis have always been a part of our experience as people within community, adverse influences from history and contemporary culture have diminished the meaning of that experience. Contemporary market-driven values that devalue people and creation severely threaten any desire to practice intentional care for creation and relationships within community. African belief affirms that spiritual concern must outweigh the drive for material gain. The wages of sin (sins of abuse, disregard, overconsumption) bring death. It was precisely this abundant provision of God that propelled the Western world into the turbulent trade of human flesh, the exploration of land, exploitation of human beings, and conquest of material goods. Across three continents and over a period of five hundred years, the violations of people and land were systematically conducted under the sign of the cross. The rest is history, if one chooses to accept the human version of God's story.

The dynamic movement of God that undergirds African belief and that was sustained within African-American Christian belief moves with us even now into a new century. Through our intentional renewing of our minds and reappropriation of culture, God shows up with new opportunities for the recovery of the sacred in our life. During a time of tremendous challenge within our communities, within the social and moral crises faced by our youth across the country and the world, there is an awesome opportunity to move intentionally from praise and celebration in the sanctuary, to praxis and committed service in the community. Consistent with African and Christian belief, God's purposes are best served when human beings are actively engaged in the saving works of God, sustaining and restoring people broken off from the whole and restoring a fragmented creation to its original condition of wholeness. There is no contradiction or compromise to either Christian faith or doctrine in the reappropriation of the spirit of African belief. As a people attempting to recover from the ravages of history and the deliberate destruction of fundamentally healing beliefs, the opportunities for the reweaving of a new story are enormous. We can respond joyously to God's call to faithful action. We can reclaim a new sense of purposefulness as we learn to appreciate the spiritual wisdom evident in many of our ancient cultural beliefs, our folk literature, music, and art. This too becomes praxis that is applied to God's higher good.

Christ meets us where we are. And where we find ourselves now is in deep crisis that can only be resolved through an intentional commitment to renewal, redefinition and Spirit-filled, newly empowered activity. Spirit-driven, whole-person, whole-faith community activity within the African American church can move dynamically from the pulpit to the pew, into the streets of our communities. Such heightened activity offers us new insight into the meaning of the expression *full gospel*. The praxis of praise is a full-scale engagement of the Holy Spirit in service to all manner of brokenness: rehabilitation of the drug addict through innovative, spiritually meaningful programs; the empowerment of men and women to reclaim the beauty and purpose of life and loving relationships; the care and nurturance of children through activity that takes crime and drugs from the streets and brings love back to the family and schools; the provision of training and employment to men and women who courageously try to move from welfare to work; the provision of caring homes and programs that watch over children while their parents try to transform their lives; the empowerment of men and women as they revitalize their neighborhoods and build decent housing; the reduction of the numbers among us who get sick and die prematurely due to inadequate health care or lack or food; the elimination of hazardous, polluted environments near playgrounds and housing; the designing of programs for our elderly that honor and cultivate their gifts. This is praxis that flows from proclamation and praise. Full gospel is nothing less than intentional, holistic worshipful action and witness that heals persons and restores God's creation. The reappropriation of African beliefs that fill in the missing gaps of our psychospiritual history and consciousness will be threatening to some, but it can introduce new meaning for us all. The challenges are clear and the work is plentiful. God calls upon our faithful resolve to bring new hope for such a time as this. And our ancestors smile.

Praise God from whom all blessings flow, as we recover the sacred in our history, in each other and in everyday life.

Notes

1. Henry H. Mitchell, *Black Beliefs in America and West Africa* (New York: Harper & Row, 1997). See an early exploration into this topic by Henry H. Mitchell in *Black Preaching* (New York: Harper & Row, 1979), 32–35. For a more contemporary discussion see also Robert Hood, *Must God Remain Greek? Afro Cultures and God Talk* (Minneapolis: Fortress, 1990), 13–76.

2. Refer to Edward Wilmont Blyden, "Christianity and the Negro Race," in the excellent anthology *African Intellectual Heritage*, ed. Moefi Asante and Albu S. Abarry (Philadelphia: Temple University Press, 1996), 477–82.

3. See John S. Mbiti, *African Religion and Philosophy*, 2d rev. and enl. ed. (Oxford: Heinemann, 1990). See also *African Ideas of God: A Symposium*, ed. E. G. Parrinder (London: Edinburgh House, 1966), 1–75.

4. For a discussion of contextual knowing, see Walter Brueggemann, *Texts Under Negotiation* (Minneapolis: Fortress, 1993), 6–18.

5. See Kwesi Dickson and Paul Ellingworth, *Biblical Revelation and African Beliefs* (Maryknoll, N.Y.: Orbis, 1969), 17–46.

6. A thorough discussion is included in the chapter "Religion and Ideology" in Marimba Ani, *Yurugu: An African-Centered Critique of European Cultural Thought and Behavior* (Trenton, N.J.: Africa World Press, Inc., 1994), 109–97.

7. Ibid., 190. See also the chapter "Conquest and Cultural Contact in the

New World" in Charles H. Long, *Significations: Signs, Symbols, and Images in the Interpretation of Religion* (Aurora, Colo.: The Davies Group, 1999), 107–24.

8. See Dwight N. Hopkins and George C. L. Comings, eds., *Cut Loose Your Stammering Tongue* (Maryknoll, N.Y.: Orbis, 1991), 4.

9. Theophus H. Smith, *Conjuring Culture: Biblical Formations of Black America* (New York and Oxford: Oxford University Press, 1994), 212–18.

10. Ibid., 57.

11. Melville J. Herskovits, *The New World Negro* (Bloomington and London: Indiana University Press, 1966), 168–70.

12. For this discussion see C. G. Baëta, "Lecture on Amos and Liberation Theology," unpublished notes from Danquah Memorial Lecture, Accra, 1981.

13. Janheinz Jahn, *Muntu: African Culture and the Western World* (New York: Grove Weidenfeld, 1990), 104–6.

14. For an in-depth discussion of ancestors in African culture, see Jomo Kenyatta, *Facing Mount Kenya* (New York: Vintage, 1962).

15. See Jocelyn Godwin, *Harmonies of Heaven and Earth* (New York: Inner Traditions International, 1987). For a discussion of the religious context of African rhythms, see John Miller Chernoff, *African Rhythm and African Sensibility* (Chicago and London: University of Chicago Press, 1979), 140–42.

16. Ted Andrews, *Sacred Sounds* (St. Paul, Minn.: Llewellyn, 1993), 89–98. For a further discussion of Hebrew orality in the transmission of the Torah, see Rabbi David A. Copper, *God Is a Verb* (New York: Riverhead, 1997), 15–19.

17. Jahn, chap. 5.

18. Henry H. Mitchell, *Celebration and Experience in Preaching* (Nashville: Abingdon, 1990), 17–18.

19. Hopkins, 7.

20. John Janzen, "The Tradition of Renewal in Kongo Religion," in *African Religions: A Symposium*, ed. Newell S. Booth Jr. (New York, London, and Lagos: NOK, 1977), 107.

CHAPTER 8

WOMEN AND PREACHING
Telling the Story in Our Own Voice

PATRICIA A. GOULD-CHAMP

Anyone who is remotely familiar with Henry and Ella Mitchell is aware of the fact that they are a gifted ministry team. But while gifted and a team in every sense of word, as preachers they are as different and unique as day and night. And it is this fact that causes them to be such a strong preaching team, the likes of which we have not seen in the twentieth century. Ella Mitchell, the female member of this dynamic preaching duo, brings that special brand of femaleness to preaching that causes the preaching moment to become a unique salvific event. And once again we are forced to examine the fact that there is a quality that women bring to the preaching moment that is powerful, unique, and mysterious at the same time.

I believe this work that strives to honor the Mitchells for their great contribution to the ministry in general and preaching in particular gives us a rare opportunity to examine the unique gifts of women as preachers. No one can deny that Ella Mitchell's books, *Those Preaching Women* (vols. 1, 2, and 3), have forever shaped public opinion with regard to women as preachers. But what is this preaching quality that defies definition and is being used to bless and shape the contemporary church? How do these preaching qualities relate to issues of gender justice and authority in the church? Do women communicate differently in the pulpit as compared with men? Do women use personal experiences and illustrations differently in the pulpit as compared with men? What do women bring to the preaching moment that makes the experience unique? I hope to examine Women and Preaching: The Language; Women and Preaching: The Substance; Women and Preaching: The Style; and Women and Preaching: The Struggle.

100

WOMEN AND PREACHING: THE LANGUAGE

It is difficult, if not impossible, to separate the language of women preachers from an examination of issues of gender justice. For our language generally denotes our journey and our struggle. For not only does language express who we are, but also it is an expression of culture. This point is often missed by those who dismiss the importance of inclusive language. For those who are privileged to be included, inclusive language often becomes optional and irrelevant. But for women who have suffered oppression and exclusion even in the church, inclusive language is an issue of justice:

> In other words, the male bias of our culture is carried in its language, and inclusive language is a moral issue; it is a matter of justice. When we fail to use gender inclusive language, we deny equal importance to women and men, and perpetuate a culture which discriminates against women, and in which none of us is whole because of it.[1]

While there is evidence that women preachers tend to use more inclusive language, there is still some confusion as to what constitutes inclusive language. Is it exclusively language concerning God, or does it also include the language used in addressing the hearers? Regardless, women are prone to be more intentional about the use of inclusive language. In fact, according to Cheryl Sanders, language may be the most distinguishing quality with regard to women as preachers as compared to their male counterparts:

> The fourth analytical category applied to the sermon sample was the use of inclusive language. As might be expected, the men were far less likely than the women to use words like *he, his,* and *father* with references to God, and to speak of people in general as man or mankind in their sermons. In fact, the majority of women and the minority of men used inclusive language in both cases.[2]

But beyond inclusive language, women preachers have a unique language. The unique quality of this language is born out of the woman's struggle against oppression and experiences of being ostracized. Women tend to use the inclusive language of *we* and *us* versus the exclusive language of *you* and *they*. This personal touch with regard to language gives women preachers a unique bond with their hearers and therefore allows the message to be received at a very personal level that is profound and mystical. The language of women preachers is deeper than words but is the language of those who share in the struggle to be and to become. This is especially true for some African American women preachers who are not nearly as concerned about gender-inclusive language as are white feminists. Rather, the language of African American women preachers today is akin to the language of African American womanist theologians. Delores Williams, in *Sisters in the Wilderness*, characterizes womanist theology as follows:

> Womanist theology attempts to help black women see, affirm and have confidence in the importance of their experience and faith for determining the character of the Christian religion in the African American community. Womanist theology challenges all oppressive forces impeding black women's struggle for survival and for the development of a positive, productive quality of life conducive to woman's and the family's freedom and well-being. Womanist theology opposes all oppression based on race, class, sexual preference, physical disability, and caste.[3]

This language allows women to move beyond the limitations of race and gender and to be committed to the survival of and wholeness of entire people, male and female. The language of women speaks a word of hope to a larger group of people to include men, women, and families. The language of womanist theology is not so much liberation as it is survival. And there is a vast difference. According to Williams, the task of the womanist theologian is

> to show black woman their salvation does not depend upon any form of surrogacy made sacred by traditional and orthodox understandings of Jesus' life and death. Rather, their salvation is assured by Jesus' life resistance and by the survival strategies he used to help people survive.[4]

Survival language forces us to reexamine God's saving activity among those who are still oppressed and abused. Liberation language, on the other hand, may be inadequate for those who are still hanging on, waiting and, for all purposes, not healed. And this language of survival causes us to identify with our sisters in the struggle to the extent that inclusive language takes on more than an exercise in the proper use of words but rather becomes an issue of ownership of oneness in suffering. In fact, this language of survival allows women preachers to include themselves in the experiences of groups other than women without being offensive to those groups. For women preachers have the ability to find credibility with other sufferers regardless of race and gender. That is why it is not unusual for men and children, as well as other women, to be blessed by the preaching of women. The oppressed understand the language of a fellow sufferer and the word of hope that they bring becomes truth.

Women preachers are able to convey in their being a suffering Christ who takes upon himself the cares of the world. And nobody knows about the suffering of women like Jesus. He is the one who cares and who ultimately is the source of empowerment. Yes, African American women can identify with this Jesus and are able to preach about him with authority. We are the embodiment of a suffering Christ who takes upon himself the concerns of the world. This is the day-to-day existence of women, especially African American women. The language of women preachers is as much being as it is words. The language of women preachers is as much what she says as who she be. Katie Geneva Cannon in *Black Womanist Ethics* names three primary qualities that describe African American women: invisible dignity, quiet grace, and unshouted courage.[5]

WOMEN AND PREACHING: THE SUBSTANCE

We preach the gospel as we have experienced it in our daily lives. With this in mind, is the substance of women's preaching different from that of men? Overall, there do not appear to be vast differences in the preaching substance of men and women. But at least one study examines the themes of preaching for women and men. Men tended to preach on the church and its mission while themes particular to women's preaching tended to be survival, healing, and ministry.[6] And that makes sense given the fact that men tend to be pastors and in leadership positions where the church and its mission is the focal concern. Because women, for the most part, do not find themselves in leadership roles that place the direction of the mission of the church under their direct responsibility, they do not tend to spend a lot of energy on doctrinal issues or corrective sermons. Women, as opposed to men, often find themselves in assistance roles of ministry alongside other members of the congregation. These roles tend to put them in closer touch with the daily plight of the congregants, especially with regard to problems and concerns. Thus their preaching reflects a greater sensitivity to those in need of survival and healing.

When we look at the lives of black women, survival is the order of the day versus liberation and/or feminism, ideologies more closely associated with white women. In fact, for the African American woman preacher, a feminist perspective in preaching is not a common occurrence. What tends to be a common thread in African American women's preaching is a concern for justice not only for themselves but also for all oppressed people.

The substance of preaching for women is more closely aligned to womanist theology. For womanist theologians have helped us with their reexamination of familiar biblical texts as they relate to women's issues. The liberation themes are inadequate for women, especially African American women. Our existence for the most part is one of survival, not liberation. According to Williams in *Sisters in the Wilderness*, as women we speak the language of those still in the wilderness versus those who have reached the exodus.[7] In other words, the woman preacher has the task of preaching to people, especially women, who are going through and who have no view of the light at the end of the tunnel. And because many of the women preachers, if not all, are also going through, we understand the journey, and that is the substance of our preaching. We in essence preach simultaneously our own pain and possibility. The hermeneutical principle for womanist theology offered by Jacquelyn Grant is that "the Bible must be read and interpreted in the light of Black women's own experience of oppression and God's revelation within that context."[8] And this is the substance of survival and survival preaching. The substance of survival preaching does not discount the value of the journey. Also, it does not move us to celebrate too quickly the conclusion of the journey. In fact, the substance of preaching for women is to examine the activity of God in the meantime. And it dares us to face the reality that sometimes God is silent, nonresponsive, and yes, less than a liberator. But the good news is that even this silent, nonresponsive God can bring healing and wholeness. The substance of women's preaching is struggle, survival, healing and wholeness. For the substance of our preaching is the substance of who we are as women. But beyond us, it is the substance of our people. Smith sees this as a challenge for relevant preaching by women:

> For many women preachers who minister from within these communities of struggle and resistance, survival may be a central reality of human experience that is deeply acknowledged and understood. This is the starting place for relevant and vital preaching. For women preachers who minister from within communities of social and economic privilege, struggle and survival become compelling and indicting categories of human experience that have the power to reshape proclamation.[9]

The substance of women's preaching is found in the fact that women are more prone to embrace the notion of hermeneutical suspicion in their encounters with the biblical texts. And womanist theologians have recently challenged us to revisit our traditional and orthodox theories of atonement and think not of the suffering and death of Jesus as a source of redemption but rather of his teaching, healing, and resistance as instructive for redemption.[10]

Women strive to see beyond the highly patriarchal language of the Bible and male-orientated interpretation of the commentaries. Women can preach between the lines. We can ask the questions that go unasked but that women, and all who are oppressed, find of great importance. Familiar texts like those dealing with Vashti and the woman at the well take on new meaning and are devoid of the gross misunderstanding and sexual innuendo often associated with the male treatment of the texts. The substance of women's preaching finds heroines and stories of hope in the plight of Hagar and the daughters of Lot. And of course, no one can truly tell Gomer's story but a woman. The substance of women's preaching is in our story. And it is in the story that women find their voice. The voice of women preachers is the ability to confront and comfort at the same time. The voice or substance of women's preaching is the ability to speak to people who are oppressed, hurting, and violated but who are nonetheless required to maintain and live from day to day. Women preachers help us to name our reality and to find hope in the midst. It would be fair to say that women weave the substance of their sermons out of the substance of their lives. Women see the text differently and therefore preach it differently. The images of God and women in the biblical texts are presented in ways that shock, challenge, and yes, anger those who have become comfortable with the given. The substance of women's preaching is freshness and the ability to make us look around and discover where we are as a people. This substance challenges those who have become comfortable but it serves to release in those of us in the wilderness a spirit of hope.

WOMEN AND PREACHING: THE STYLE

How do women develop their style of preaching? Who are their models? Is there a distinctive female style of preaching? All of these questions are unanswered at this time, and there are few substantive studies to help us. However, the style of preaching for women is a critical issue as more women than ever are being called to preach and are finding themselves in homiletics classes at major seminaries all over the country. In a 1984 Association of Theological Schools research grant conducted by Edwina Hunter, in which thirteen homiletics professors from ten selected seminaries were asked to assess women preachers, it was reported that women were making the highest percentage of A grades in preaching.[11] It appears that women preachers are proving themselves to be awesome preachers who are developing a style all their own. But how do women develop their style for preaching? Women preachers, like all preachers, develop their preaching style from preachers they have heard, been taught by, or served under. And since it has been difficult if not impossible to find female role models in these capacities, many women have been forced to model male preachers. Sometimes this has led to the use of ridiculous male mannerisms in the pulpit such as loosening the collar, lifting or kicking the leg, and cupping the ear with one hand. The good news is that it appears that fewer persons of either gender are seriously attempting to imitate older, more established, or well-known preachers.[12]

According to Miles Jones, homiletics professor at the Samuel DeWitt Proctor School of Theology, a sermon is a statement of faith that gives evidence of the authenticity of the messenger. And no one can be authentic like the black preacher. Henry Mitchell in *Black Preaching* states: "From its earliest beginnings Black preaching has been clearly characterized by great emphasis on personal style or individual variations. About the most certain statement one can make about Black preaching style is that *nothing* is certain or fixed."[13]

Authenticity and style are important for the preacher. And women preachers are daring to develop their own style and in so doing are challenging their male counterparts to do the same. For women preachers, their style encompasses the total look. This includes how they look when they approach the preaching moment. So women are daring to move beyond the traditional black male-oriented robes that are hot and ill-fitting. They have opted for more colorful, symbol-laden, light-weight, flowing robes that enhance the worship service and force the worshiper to see the preacher in her authentic female self. As a worshiper once said to me, "Anybody who dares to wear red in the pulpit has to have a 'serious' word." Women are daring to preach in their authentic being, which may include a soft voice, conversational tone, and engaging eye contact. Women are finding the mannerisms that are comfortable for them and in so doing are finding a comfortable blend of what they have received from male preachers. This blended style has produced many great women preachers who whoop, tune, and otherwise celebrate in the traditional African-American preaching style.

Women approach the task of preaching more in the spirit of relationship than competition. The joy is in sharing what has been prepared. In fact, most women enjoy sermon preparation, recognizing the importance of scholarly exegesis. Women tend to be more concerned about what they say versus how it is said. In recent years, women have begun to give more attention to sermon delivery, and this has made their preaching stronger. Although there are no conclusive studies, women tend to have a more didactic style of preaching. The goal seems to be to make the sermon as simple as possible, allowing it to be understood by both adults and young people. This unique style is difficult to master, but women preachers seem to possess it as an innate gift.

In Sanders's article she reports that women sought to accomplish a greater variety of tasks in preaching and that it appears that story telling and testifying were generally more important to women preachers than to the men.[14] This seems to be a part of the unique style of women preachers. Women tend to be more transparent in their preaching and use more personal references in their preaching. Women's preaching is more likely to include their personal testimony of faith and personal references about their family. Women tend to emphasize the personal and men the prophetic.[15] The style of women is diverse and mystical — it involves dress, mannerisms, voice, and content. The style is emerging and elusive. The best thing that can be said about the style of women preachers is that it is captured in her womanhood. And this is creating a style that cannot be duplicated.

It is an understatement to say that all women preachers do not preach alike. And if you ask each church that has a woman preacher to assess her preaching they will all proclaim to have the best "woman preacher" in the world. This is the crux of the struggle for the women preacher. How does she move from being a "woman preacher" to being a preacher? Whenever a woman preacher stands, she is generally given the task of representing all women preachers. Therefore she is not afforded the opportunity to have a bad day or in preacher vernacular to flunk. Women cannot, nor do they desire, to be held accountable for the preaching gifts of all of their sisters. Nor do they wish to be compared with their fellow women preachers. For women do not view preaching as competitive. In fact, women tend to talk over their sermons before preaching them, and it is not unusual for women to hold a roundtable with other women about a particular passage of Scripture prior to preaching. *—men do as well*

WOMEN AND PREACHING: THE STRUGGLE

The struggle for women is within and without. Because women often suffer with issues of self-esteem and self-confidence, they discount their gifts in preaching. Women are rarely satisfied with their preaching and are constantly striving to improve in the area of preaching. The struggle within also involves the finding of one's authentic preaching self. The good news is that women no longer have to rely on male models for preaching. There are qualified and gifted women preachers in both the church and seminary arena. This is a blessing for women who have never had an opportunity to be blessed by the preaching of other women. But with highly visible and powerful contemporary women preachers like Vashti McKenzie, Ann Lightner-Fuller, Barbara Amos, and Susan Johnson-Cook, just to name a few, it is easy for women to discount who they are and opt to duplicate what these women bring to preaching. The struggle is to find one's authentic self and not settle for being a poor duplicate of others. For many women preachers seem limited by their models for preaching: diva, lecturer, whooper. But regardless of the models, McKenzie makes the point: "A woman in the pulpit represents a lot of changes for herself as well as for the congregation. She may represent the congregation's first experience of hearing a woman preach, teach, serve communion, or preside over rituals and board meetings."[16]

And with this in mind, that first impression becomes a lasting impression for that congregation and goes a long way in making a positive statement with regard to women as preachers. Every woman preacher understands the importance of being a good steward over our preaching opportunities. We know that to fail to do so does not guarantee us another chance to make the correction. Another struggle for the woman preacher is to be a woman, even in the pulpit. This involves dress, makeup, hair, and other cosmetic things. The task is not to make the mistake of forsaking our feminine self in order to be heard. I believe in recent years women preachers are doing a better job of this. In fact, women's pulpit attire is becoming a fast-growing business venture. Every conference is full of vendors that cater to the needs of women preachers—ranging from the demure to the flamboyant. Gone are the days of women dressed in black with no makeup and big hats. Women are daring to be their feminine, beautiful selves. However, the present challenge for women preachers is much greater. It is the challenge to be heard above who we are as women. In other words, is it possible for women to be seen in all their feminine glory but not to the extent that they are not seen solely as preacher? In other words, is it possible to be seen as a woman and not seen as a woman at the same time? That is the ultimate challenge. That no one be able to deny that there is a woman in the pulpit but, at the preaching moment, be oblivious to the fact that a woman is preaching. Every woman preacher I know wants to hear that she is a good preacher versus she is a good woman preacher.

The struggle for the woman preacher is to be faithful to sermon preparation. This does not appear to be an issue initially when opportunities are limited. But as women receive more opportunities to preach, there may be a temptation to take shortcuts and to use the antics modeled by some of their male counterparts—singing, joke telling, and the like. The struggle for the woman preacher is to always have done the best scholarly preparation possible. If given a choice, one can never go wrong when the content of the sermon is geared toward excellence.

As always, the struggle for men and women is to operate within our authentic gifts. For women, this entails being comfortable with one's own preaching voice regardless of the tone quality. And being comfortable means not forcing one's voice to operate in ways that strain and become unnatural or awkward. The struggle for women is to develop mannerisms that are natural and feminine. Also, what mannerisms are necessary? Too often, some mannerisms have become habitual and their original intent has been lost. I hope women preachers will not fall prey to this trap.

Finally, the struggle for women preachers is to accept their gifts as a preacher and to share those preaching gifts comfortably and with authority. For preaching is liberating, and as women preachers preach, they are freed by the preachment. The struggle is within and without. Women preachers must be true to themselves and not allow others to push them to be inauthentic. As women are able to resist this temptation, they will develop their own style and come forth as powerful, prophetic preachers. The struggle continues, and women preachers are holding their own and in most cases excelling.

As we conclude this work on women and preaching, we give honor to Ella Mitchell, who was honored at the 1999 Hampton

Ministers Conference as the mother of women preachers. She continues to represent that caliber of woman preacher who has a style all her own. She is the epitome of the preacher who receives the Word and brings that word forth in the totality of who she is as a woman. Ella Mitchell reminds us of the wonderful thing God has done in calling women to preach. She challenges preachers, women and men alike, to offer no less than our best. For this we are eternally thankful. She is the best of *Those Preachin' Women!*

BIBLIOGRAPHY

Books

Cannon, Katie Geneva. *Black Womanist Ethics.* Atlanta: Scholars Press, 1988.
Farmer, David, and Edwina Hunter, eds. *And Blessed Is She: Sermons by Women.* Valley Forge, Pa.: Judson, 1990.
Grant, Jacquelyn. *White Women's Christ and Black Women's Jesus: Feminist Christology and Womanist Response.* Atlanta: Scholars Press, 1989.
McKenzie, Vashti M. *Not Without a Struggle: Leadership Development for African American Women in Ministry.* Cleveland: United Church Press, 1996.
Mitchell, Henry H. *Black Preaching.* New York: Harper & Row, 1979.
Moody, Linda A. *Women Encounter God: Theology Across the Boundaries of Difference.* Maryknoll, N.Y.: Orbis, 1996.
Williams, Delores. *Sisters in the Wilderness: The Challenge of Womanist God-Talk.* Maryknoll, N.Y.: Orbis, 1993.

Articles

Sanders, Cheryl. "The Woman as Preacher." *The Journal of Religious Thought* 43, no. 1 (spring/summer 1986): 6–23.
Smith, Christine. "Women Preachers." *Word and World* 15, no. 3 (summer 1995): 326–30.

NOTES

1. Jonathan F. Moody, "Thinking About Language, Community and Inclusion," *Church Educator* 16, no. 11 (November 1990): 27.

2. Cheryl J. Sanders, "The Woman as Preacher," *The Journal of Religious Thought* 43, no. 1 (spring/summer 1986): 6.

3. Delores Williams, *Sisters in the Wilderness: The Challenge of Womanist God-Talk* (Maryknoll, N.Y.: Orbis, 1993), xiv.

4. Ibid., 164.

5. Katie Geneva Cannon, *Black Womanist Ethics* (Atlanta: Scholars Press, 1988), 10.

6. Sanders, 9.

7. Williams, 144.

8. Jacquelyn Grant, *White Women's Christ and Black Women's Jesus: Feminist Christology and Womanist Response* (Atlanta: Scholars Press, 1989), 212.

9. Christine M. Smith, "Women Preachers," *Word and World* 15, no. 3 (summer 1995): 326.

10. Williams, 162.

11. David Albert Farmer and Edwina Hunter, eds., *And Blessed Is She: Sermons by Women* (Valley Forge, Pa.: Judson, 1990), 90.

12. Ibid.

13. Henry H. Mitchell, *Black Preaching* (New York: Harper & Row, 1979), 162.

14. Sanders, 21.

15. Ibid., 22.

16. Vashti M. McKenzie, *Not Without a Struggle: Leadership Development for African American Women in Ministry* (Cleveland: United Church Press, 1996), 64.

CHAPTER 9

RETEXTURIZATION OF A TRADITION
A Womanist Hermeneutical Complex
for Understanding the Religio-Historical Value
of the African American Sermonic Genre

ALISON P. GISE JOHNSON

Due to limited use of sources and less than critical methods of analysis, the religious histories of African American women preachers have been invisibilized,[1] distorted, and relegated to the position of exhibition.[2] The messages and experiences of black women who preached have been decontextualized. As a result, they have become two-dimensional, lifeless, monolithic presentations to be observed, but they have not been utilized to inform and reconstruct the history of the African American Christian community(ies) and the society at large. Therefore African American religious history has been stripped of the complexities of its texture.

Thus this necessitates the use of new sources[3] and methods of inquiry and analysis to retexture the histories and experiences of black women who preached and of those to whom they preached. Retexturization is a critical iterative process that reintroduces the complexities of human history by interfacing noncanonical sources and analytical tools with traditional research methods in order to raise critical questions and to converge on original contexts and meanings, such that women's participation in religious history is not generated through imaginative interpretations of others. Rather, through the clarity of a face-to-face stance, women are recorded as agents of history and culture generating their own images while at the same time critiquing institutionalized image makers.

113

In this chapter I will:

argue for the import of African American sermons as genre and source
for the purpose of historical inquiry; develop a methodological means of
inquiry and analysis that can be used in the process of retexturization of
traditions as applied to the sermons of the Reverend Florence Spearing
Randolph and the experiences of the Reverend Sarah Potter Smith;

use an autobiographical interview[4] to extract complexities of experiences of
a preacher who simultaneously exists in the mainstream and on the margin;

and analyze both the sermons and autobiographical interview for their
theo-ethical positioning.

SERMONS AS SOURCES FOR HISTORICAL RESEARCH

Recently the sermons of African American women have been com-
piled in order to chronicle the presence of African American women
in what historically has been the most powerful position within
black communities and churches, the role of preacher.[5] Many of
the sermons have been posited as apologetics and responses to
the "invisibilization" of women in collections of "the best black
sermons."[6] Such efforts will continue as long as black women
preaching is seen as a new thing, an exception or exhibition. And
the historical import of the sermonic tradition will be overlooked.

The collection and preservation of all black sermons by both
African American women and men, especially those dated before the middle of the twentieth century, represent something far
greater than apologetic materials to prove the presence and capabilities of women as ministers or the powerful and artistic style
ascribed to black male preachers. Represented in these sources is
a repository of information to be used for historical restoration.
Sermons represent the beginnings of articulation of definitive statements about theological developments and ethical positioning of
African American communities in the face of racism, oppression,
wars, and continual formations and assimilation. African American preachers who have wrestled with and delivered these sermons
have held a particular prophetic stance that is representative of the
articulation and development of prescriptive liberation preaching
and resistance to cultural and economic annihilation.

These prophetic articulations are cultural productions that pre-serve dimensions of the religious life of a particular community. Within this genre are elements that connect the experiences of the community with the environment and elements of larger societies. Preserved within the sermonic traditions are reflections on social and moral struggles as well as prophetic messages of resistance, lib-eration, and character formation.[7] For every religious community, there are historical writings that serve as a text for extracting essen-tial elements of community concerns and struggles. The content of these text are an indication of what is going on in a community in response to external pressures, what is not going on internally that may be a hindrance to the community of faith, and what should be going on in response to divine activity. Therefore, the sermon is both lively and liberative — pointing to ways beyond the restric-tions presented as institutionalized power and culturized reality. Thus the sermon serves to invite the listening community to re-ceive forms of resistance by bringing both comfort and discomfort simultaneously. This tradition as "the spoken representation of the dimensions of the holy is divine activity wherein the word of God is proclaimed or announced concerning contemporary issues with a view toward ultimate response to God."[8]

In addition to the content of sermons being indications of religious and social developments, the form or structural presen-tation of sermons also provides indicators used for determining historical trends in theological reflection, ethical formation, and rhetorical methodologies.[9] The intrinsic character of sermons, therefore, provides a multiplicity of data that can be used for developing or reconstructing histories of communities. This can be illustrated in the text of the Christian and Jewish Scriptures as they have been used for reconstructing the socioeconomic his-tories as well as theological developments of the communities represented in these writings.[10] In light of this, the sermons of African American preachers are not to be considered only as an art form, as some might suggest due to the animated presenta-tion or style. When they are considered as sources for historical inquiry, sermons of African American liberation preachers rep-resent an element of texture fundamental to African American faith communities and theo-ethical developments particular to the cultural contexts.

Methodological Approaches to Source Analysis

As the types of sources increase and the questions posed to the source take on new dimensions, means of analysis must also be formulated. In the past, the analysis particular to black women's history has been inadequate. It has been done using what Rosalynn Terborg-Penn calls the "white filter."[11] Analysis from this perspective results in distorted histories that allow the "researchers to manipulate the interpretations of the data in order to fulfill their search for pathologies, deficiencies and passive responses of blacks and then posit such as the norm and the bases for exhibition." Lives of black women cannot be fully comprehended using analytical categories derived from white/male perspectives. Often times such concepts covertly sustain "a hierarchy of white supremacy, patriarchy and exploitative power."[12] Therefore, more accurate and complex analytical methods must be utilized to correct the distortions and truncated scholarship of the past.

For this study I have developed and will use the womanist hermeneutical complex, which is a combination of three methodological approaches for analytical purposes. The first component of the complex is what is considered to be traditional biblical exegetical process. Exegesis is a systematic way of interpreting the text without deeming it necessary to establish the meaning of the text. Within this method is the recognition that the exact meaning of the text cannot be extracted, but elements of communication of the text may be exposed by understanding the relationship of various factors that are involved in the communication process. These factors are illustrated in the following schematic diagram:[13]

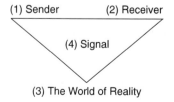

The exegesis is a two-step process that utilizes analysis and then synthesis. The task of analysis separates the passage into its component parts and problems and examines them as discrete units and issues. The examination comes in the form of the following criticisms: textual, historical, grammatical, literary, form, tradition, redaction, and structural.[14] The second step of the exegetical process is a synthesis in which the text is put back together. At this stage the task is to relate the preliminary analytical investigations to each other, weighing the significance of each and deciding how they contribute to the interpretation of the text as a whole.

The second component of the womanist hermeneutical complex takes into consideration not only the text but also seeks to use the text to move beyond the text. This is the process of human archaeology[15] that "seeks to uncover the layers of mask and inhibition in search of a more authentic representation of life experiences by recognizing, utilizing and legitimating the questions and suspicions raised out of the historian's own consciousness." This component of the method stands juxtaposed to traditional research in its purported objectivity. Human archaeology draws from the interests and the passions of the interpreter and uses them as a catalyst for inquiry. This method of analysis adds to the process of re-texturization of black women's histories by insisting on studying not only the tangible historical artifacts but also the distinctive consciousness related to the experiences and institutions of black women. Human archaeology as it is used from a womanist perspective seeks to "comprehend how Black women create their own lives, influence others and understand themselves as a force in their own right."[16]

The third component of the complex is the womanist hermeneutic,[17] which is an interpretive tool used to expose and analyze elements of liberation as they relate to the complexity of race, class, and gender analysis. This analysis is used specifically for the critique of black sermonic text. At the vortex of this methodological approach is uncovering and valuing theo-ethical positioning as an indicator of oppressive or liberating interpretations of Scripture, images of women, and participation in sociopolitical practices.

The sources and methodologies are combined in order to begin in some senses a discussion of the complexity of what has been a simplified and often romanticized perception of black preaching, the previously muted or superficially spiritualized messages of women in ministry, and the realities of experiences of women in the ministry. In addition, these methodologies are combined as a multidimensional crosscheck such that the interest or analysis associated with each component is kept in balance. Iteratively interfaced sources and analysis methodologies, as represented in this womanist hermeneutical complex, mandates new questions being asked and new sources being added in order to verify interpretations with continued convergence on original *Sitz im Leben,* or situations in life.

"His Eye Is on the Sparrow":[18]
The Experiences and Theology of
the Reverend Dr. Sarah Potter Smith

Dr. Sarah Potter Smith tells the story of her aunt, who was a church vocalist. One Sunday during service she sang the hymn "His Eye Is on the Sparrow," and as Smith puts it, "that song touched my little heart." That Sunday at the age of five, Sarah Potter asked her aunt to teach her that song. It was the first song that began her singing career, that became the central theme of her ministry, and presently depicts her experiences.

The Reverend Sarah Potter Smith was born Sarah Potter on April 30, 1902, in Chester, Pennsylvania. Her birth was not a perfect one. She was born with "a deformed body and a stammering tongue." Even more deadly, she had a congenital heart condition so severe that there were times as she sat, she began to cough up large quantities of blood. This led to the prognosis that she would not live to the critical age of twelve. Though she was ill most of her early years, she made it beyond the age of twelve. However, when she was nineteen, again death seemed imminent. She lay in her bed, and once again the doctors and her mother awaited her death. It was during this time, however, that Sarah Potter was called to preach:

> [T]hey [her mother and a few neighbors] were downstairs, and a light
> flashed on the wall, and there were words that said "you're not going to
> die. You're going to live and you're going to have flesh and blood," and the
> Lord came and stood at the foot of my bed and raised his hands over me
> and said "I call you to preach, I call you to preach, I call you to preach."

Sarah's official ministry did not begin until her ordination to dea-
con by the Delaware Conference of the Methodist church in 1944.
The Methodist church had been segregated since 1863 with all of
the black congregations grouped into the central district and sub-
divided by region. The Delaware Conference was the governing
body of the eastern regional black Methodist churches. It was this
body that ordained Sarah. From the conference records, the earliest mentioned ordination of a black woman was 1927. Her name
was Pearl R. Brown. At the time of Sarah Potter Smith's ordination, the Reverend Brown had been ordained elder, but she was still
listed as a supply pastor, which meant she was not the senior pastor
of a church, and even more she was being paid little if anything for
her services.[19] In addition to being underpaid, if paid at all, supply
pastors were unable to vote in the annual conference or in the lay
conferences. These factors of powerlessness were evidenced at the
1944 conference, which led to the following resolution:

> Whereas, the Supply Pastors represent one-third of the total pastors of the
> Conference, and whereas, there is no special source of revenue for regular
> distribution of relief, be it further resolved that a definite and reasonable
> amount of other funds be allocated to the Supply Pastors' Fund.
> Be it resolved, that the Annual Conference ask its General conference
> delegate to memorialize the General Conference of 1944 to permit the
> supply Pastors to vote in their own Annual Conference. or at least the Lay
> Conference of which we feel to be the legal members.[20]

During that same year, three women were ordained as local
preachers or deacons. They were Minnie Ellis, Ada V. Coffey, and
Sarah Smith. Ada Coffey became a supply pastor; Minnie Ellis
and Sarah Smith disappeared from the records. It is through the
ministry and story of Sarah Potter Smith that we gain some insight into the possible causes of the complexities associated with
invisibility. When asked what she wanted to do with her ordination, the Reverend Smith replied, "I don't know." Her decision
had two major consequences, one financial and the other moral.

The financial consequence was and is, even to the present, that the Reverend Smith, though serving as assistant pastor of Zoar United Methodist Church of Philadelphia, is not on the official payroll of the church, nor does she receive a pension.

The moral consequence was that she became autonomous. As she states, "I did not have to be under the discipline[21] of the church." As a result she was able to authentically focus on critical ministries. Contended as a primary issue at the 1944 conference was the decline in participation of youth in the church. According to the report of the board of Christian education, "next to the war, the topic of concern is juvenile delinquency. The impact of the war has both intensified the problem and dramatized it." In subsequent years the predicament was the same, but the Reverend Smith did not blame it on the war. She suggested that the Methodist church engaged in anemic efforts that had no investment in youth except for what their presence represented without provisions for valued participation within church life. Indicative of this posture was the fact of little to no resources allocated for youth ministries. In the 1944 journal, pastors were paid $59,025; general conference received $8,391; women's local work had resources of $15,024, and they sent $1,808 to the conference for women's work. However, the budget for the youth conference fund was $144.

Though the years have not been verified, it seems that during this same time, after the Reverend Smith's ordination, she preached a youth revival at Zoar church, and more than one hundred youth came to Christ. After the revival the Reverend Smith, being concerned about the youth, went to the official board of Zoar church and said:

> [N]ow what are you going to do? They said what do you think we're going to do? They're saved aren't they? I said, that's the problem, they're saved. So when they didn't have any idea, not anything to offer the young people. Not a church ministry or anything, that's when the Lord led me to take them on the air for those years [this is in reference to the youth choir named "Called Youth" that Smith started].... You have to plan to help people find themselves in the Lord, once they're saved.... And if you don't have something that you make them feel involved in or even sharing what they have with someone else, their [sic] likely to grope back where they were, again.

This incident is not only a critique of the church from the margins of the church, but it also serves as a foundation or starting point for understanding the Reverend Potter Smith's theology, anthropology, and pneumatology.[22] In her theology, the Reverend Smith talks a lot about individuals coming to God. But when she discusses her prison ministry, she talks about how God does not want the young men to be in prison, but since they are there, then God comes to them. God seems to be a God of mutuality, and in her words, "the Lord never gives up on anyone. You give up on him." The Reverend Smith's theology and anthropology are inextricably connected. Even though God knows what choices humankind will make, the choice still belongs to the human. The choice is to trust that God will operate on behalf of those who are not necessarily perfect or good, but those who trust. God does not coerce. God only provides opportunities. Closely associated with her anthropology is her pneumatology. The Holy Spirit is the power that gives endurance and justice-making potential.

While discussing her ordination and her trip to Beijing, she cites the following Scripture:

> "You shall eat in plenty and be satisfied....
> And my people shall never again be put to shame.
> You shall know that I am in the midst of Israel....
>
> "And it shall come to pass afterward,
>   that I will pour my spirit on all flesh;
> your sons and your daughters shall prophesy,
>   your old men shall dream dreams,
>   and your young men shall see visions."
>   (Joel 2:26–29, RSV)

The Scripture speaks of justice found in the restoration of the whole community, but the Reverend Potter Smith interprets the text to suggest the witness of the transformation of women and God's activity in history from her ordination to the present:

[S]ome of those women were fifty and sixty years old then [1944], and it was just amazing that they had been in the church serving and serving and had not gotten any more recognition. But they ... like the women today are coming into their own. And that's what this thing in China was about ... women.... I said we're living in the last days and we're [referring

to women] suppose to come forth. And not to gloat over men, but to be
who we are suppose to be in the Lord.

WOMAN THE BUILDER OF THE HOUSE: THE SERMONS OF THE REVEREND FLORENCE SPEARING RANDOLPH

In the sermons of the Reverend Florence Spearing Randolph, there
is evidence not only of a particular theological stance, but also
there is particular emphasis on community building and justice
making as it relates to the transformation of black women. This
transformation is not solely based on women becoming something
that they have not already been, but the change comes as men
and women, women especially, realign their experiences with pre-
designed or even historical possibilities and dispositions. Through
both the form and content of these sermons, Randolph makes definitive statements about not only the images of black women but
also the roles and responsibilities of black women and the black
community at large. This is evidenced in both the form and content
of the sermons preached by the Reverend Randolph.

The Reverend Randolph seems to follow a particular form that
may be viewed as an internally inverted Hegelian methodology.
The Hegelian[23] method is outlined as follows:

> Antithesis
>
> Thesis
>
> Relevant question
>
> Synthesis (using at least three points)

The antithesis explains the condition of existence of humanity
that is in opposition to divine design and thus leads to injustices
and distorted self-images. The thesis describes the condition that
"ought to be." "The thesis is God's answer to the antithesis,"[24]
and the relevant question brings the two into tension but more
importantly introduces the synthesis. The synthesis provides the
understanding of how the antithesis may be abandoned for the
attainment of the thesis.

In the Reverend Randolph's sermons, especially those that are
particular to women, the outline is as follows:

Thesis

Antithesis

Relevant question

Synthesis

The sermon "The Friends of Wickedness"[25] illustrates this point well:

Thesis: Some great writer on speaking of Eve the mother of the human family said, "When she received the breath of life, the work of omnipotence was finished. Nothing more remained to be done. Perfection was stamped on everything. "All was good." And then the morning stars sang together and all the sons of God shouted for joy." And thus the world loves to think of womankind as being good and tender and [perfect] gentle. . . . And we might go on to speak of Elizabeth the mother of John, or Hannah the mother of Samuel or Mary the mother of Jesus.

Antithesis: But with sorrow we must change the [scene], as the subject of the text is the daughter of a very wicked woman.

Relevant question: We desire to learn from these two wicked characters to shun sin in any and every form because sin leads to sin and the end thereof is death. Our text is "What shall I ask?"

This form and content combination suggests three things. First, the Reverend Randolph may have been familiar with the rhetorical methodologies present in the larger communities, but at the same time the methods were modified to address the particularities of an African American congregation, which was probably mostly women for this particular service. Second, it may suggest that this form is employed to affect transformation based on a larger vision rather than guilt, shame oppression, and overidentification with negative images.

Even more obvious in this sermon is the interpretation of women in the Scriptures that are used. Presently, the critique of traditional biblical interpretations by womanist theologians has been the inordinate Scripture use that characterizes African American women as "sin-bringing Eve," "wilderness-whimpering Hagar," "hen-pecking Jezebel," "whoring Gomer," "prostituting Mary Magdalene," and "conspiring Sapphira."[26] Such interpretations have led to the legitimized oppression of women, especially in the church. But as the Scripture use of the Reverend Randolph between 1898 and 1946 is analyzed, it raises the question of the historicity of stereotypes of women, at least in the African American community.

In addition to the historical question of stereotypes, there is also the question of the use of sequestered space. Traditionally, the African American church has been used as an arena outside of the gaze of mainline institutionalized power structures.[27] It has been the place where the transforming activity of liberation is initiated. It would seem that the Reverend Randolph would use this space to build the downtrodden women attending these services. However, it has been observed through the internally inverted Hegelian method that this is not the case. In many of the Reverend Randolph's sermons the central contention is not the portrayal of women but more the betrayal of young women and how that relates to not only external oppression but also internal issues of class and gender oppression.[28] Intrinsic to this theme is that the African American Christian church community was facing a crisis with young women at the vortex. This condition translated according to Reverend Randolph as a crisis for the progress of the entire race. The catalyst for this crisis was not the inherent immorality of young women but the internal and external factors that served as the threshold to immoral behavior and the foundation for their antithetical condition. That is, externally, injustices, oppression, and economic violence exerted by white supremacist ideologies and internally, the invisibilization of their condition due to individual efforts toward racial progress through political and simplified religious means:

> The Negro with only thirty three years behind him in spite of opposition and disadvantages has in numerous cases proven himself the equal of Caucasians, still we are looked upon by some of that race as inferior and shiftless therefore we cannot afford to stop and look back at the distance we have come, but remember we must reach the top of the mountain and it can only be reached by assiduous labor. It is not enough to reach it individually nor a few receive equal rights. We must have it as a race.... The future development and progress of the Negro race is in the hands of the Negro, and if we want the condition of the race bettered, we must do something to make it better.... We must work unitedly, for

united efforts bring victories. We must not be contented simply to build churches, we must build race institutions of every kind and endeavor to support them independently.[29]

Thus Randolph expands the responsibility of the church in society by calling it to be responsible in the plurality of its social contexts. Randolph invokes an analysis of the Negro community that reflects the complexities of oppression. That is, she gives attention not only to race but also to class and gender issues. As is evidenced by the sermons preached, Randolph's theology is one in which God is active on behalf of African Americans in their struggle against racial oppression and negation: "The Negro has a history which God intends shall never be blotted out though his Caucasian brother would try to rob him of it, and bring about a problem."[30]

However, when confronting internal oppression, Randolph's theology is inextricably tied to her anthropology. In the particularities of this social context, divine intercession is secondary to human activity. That is, "God helps those who help themselves." Humans are given the power to affect change through their own activity. This activity is found in "self-abnegation" and "self-forgetfulness."[31] It must be restated that this hermeneutic is operative only in the community. To employ this stance toward the larger society is to side with the oppressor. But, when applied within the community, self-critique and corrective action are the situations to which the divine responds. This position is parallel or at least similar to the contemporary critique of black theology that was posited by Jacqueline Grant in 1979:

> Arising out of the Black Power Movement of the 1960s, Black Theology purports to take seriously the experience of the larger community's struggle for liberation. But if this is, indeed, the case, Black Theology must function in the secular community in the same way it functions in the church community. It must serve as a "self-test" to see whether the rhetoric or proclamation of the Black communities struggle for liberation is inconsistent with its practices. How does the "self-test" principle operate among the poor and the oppressed? Certainly Black Theology has spoken to some of the forms of oppression which exist within the community of the oppressed. . . . Silence on this specific issue [sexism] can only mean conformity with the status quo.[32]

Just as suggested in the writings of Grant, the Reverend Randolph thus identifies the weakness of the black church and simultaneously adds complexity and texture to the task of liberation. The sermons of Randolph suggest the necessity of a reconstructive transformation of the entire Negro race. She critiques the inner power structures based on economics and religious privilege.

CONCLUSION

As a result of the preliminary analysis of the sermons by the Reverend Florence Spearing Randolph and the experiences of the Reverend Dr. Sarah Potter Smith, new areas of texture are given first of all to the use of noncanonical sources for historical research. The sermons and autobiographical statements of African American women not only add to the increasing data base of the existence of African American women in Euro-traditional male roles, but also their lives act as cultural productions from which information about universal views may be extracted and analyzed.

These sources find worth and utility as critical methods of inquiry are developed that not only expose the distortions of white filter scholarship. They also expose the texture of the experiences of African American women in the context of the African American community. In addition, in developing these methodologies, it is important that a womanist hermeneutic is employed in order to put into place a functioning regulatory self-critique that prevents developing new distortions.

As a result of the source-analysis combination, new questions and sites of inquiry are constantly being raised. In the sermons and experiences analyzed in this chapter, questions have been raised about the effective depths of liberation preaching and ethics. In the sermons of the Reverend Florence Spearing Randolph and the experiences of the Reverend Dr. Sarah Potter Smith, the task of liberation preaching and theology not only exists as it is traditionally defined. Liberation is also thematically enhanced and used as a critique of both internal and external authority.

In the texts of these two preachers, a womanist complexion

of liberation is generated in which dimensions of self-agency are enhanced by advocacy for those who are historically silenced. In the ministry of the Reverend Sarah Potter Smith, this is evidenced in her actions beyond the vision and efforts of the Methodist church. With ten dollars she starts a choir that stays on the air for well over five years. The critique of the oppressive structure of the Methodist church was the catalyst for the Reverend Smith to resist the invitations to compromise the possibility of what for other women in the denomination were illusive privileges of ordained ministry.

In the sermons of the Reverend Florence Spearing Randolph, the liberative self-critique is accomplished through the conscientization of the women concerning an illusive place of privilege within the community, which suggests that as long as personal space is unaffected by the oppressive forces internal and external to the community, then this served as an indication of the progress of the race. For Randolph the progress of the race can be monitored only from the foundation of the sociological structure. If youth, particularly young women, are allowed to be silently betrayed, then the race will be destroyed.

In both of the life texts analyzed, these women bring complexity and different complexion to contemporary prescriptive liberation preaching and ethics. The poor are not defined by a self-centered introspective inventory of oppression and racist structures, but the prophetic realization of liberation emerged to critique the foundations of ecclesiastical and social oppression that found as footing the youth of the African American community. In many senses, the theo-ethical articulations of these women serve as predecessors of the present womanist approaches to liberation that not only hold the lives of women of color at the vortex of transformation; their vision and investment extends to the entire African American community with special emphasis on those who are not even given the illusive privilege of being exhibited but are silenced — the youth.

Bibliography

Bailey, Randall C. *David in Love and War: The Pursuit of Power in 2 Samuel 10–12*. Sheffield: JSOT Press, 1990.

Bailey, Randall C., and Jacqueline Grant, eds. *The Recovery of Black Presence: An Interdisciplinary Exploration*. Nashville: Abingdon, 1995.

Battle, Michael A., ed. *Voices of Experience: Twentieth-Century Prophets Speak*. New York: Martin Luther King Fellows Press, 1985.

Boddie, Charles Emerson. *God's "Bad Boys."* Valley Forge, Pa.: Judson, 1985.

Bright, John. *A History of Israel*. 2d ed. Philadelphia: Westminster, 1972.

Baldwin, Lewis V. "Black Women and African Union Methodism, 1813–1983." *Methodist History* 21 (1982–1983): 225–37.

Cannon, Katie Geneva. *Black Womanist Ethics*. Atlanta: Scholars Press, 1988.

———. "Hitting a Straight Lick with a Crooked Stick: The Womanist Dilemma in the Development of a Black Liberation Ethic." In *Feminist Theological Ethics*, edited by Lois K. Daly, 59–76. Louisville, Ky.: Westminster/John Knox, 1994.

———. "Womanist Interpretations and Preaching in the Black Church." In *Searching the Scriptures*, edited by Elisabeth Schüssler Fiorenza, 326–37. New York: Crossroad, 1993.

Collier-Thomas, Bettye. *Daughters of Thunder: Black Women Preachers and Their Sermons, 1850–1979*. San Francisco: Jossey-Bass, 1998.

Copher, Charles. *Black Biblical Studies: An Anthology of Charles Copher Biblical and Theological Issues on the Black Presence in the Bible*. Chicago: Black Light Fellowship, 1993.

Davis Goode, Gloria. *Preachers of the Word and Singers of the Gospel: The Ministry of Women Among Nineteenth-Century African Americans*. Philadelphia: University of Pennsylvania Press, 1990.

Dodson, Jualynne. "Nineteenth-Century A.M.E. Preaching Women: Cutting Edge of Women's Inclusion in Church Polity." In *Women in New Worlds: Historical Perspectives on the Wesleyan Tradition*, edited by Hilah F. Thomas and Rosemary Skinner Keller, 1:276–89. 2 vols. Nashville: Abingdon, 1981–1982.

Felder, Cain Hope, ed. *Stony the Road We Trod: African American Biblical Interpretation*. Minneapolis: Fortress, 1991.

Gottwald, Norman K. *The Hebrew Bible: A Socio-Literary Introduction*. Philadelphia: Fortress, 1985.

Grant, Jacqueline. *White Women's Christ and Black Women's Jesus: Feminist Christology and Womanist Response*. Atlanta: Scholars Press, 1989.

———. "Black Theology and the Black Woman." In *Black Theology: A Documentary History*, vol. 1, *1966–1979*, edited by James Cone and Gayraud S. Wilmore. Maryknoll, N.Y.: Orbis, 1993.

Gray Crotwell, Helen. *Women and the Word: Sermons*. Philadelphia: Fortress, 1977.

Hayes, John H., and Carl R. Holladay. *Biblical Exegesis: A Beginner's Handbook*. Atlanta: John Knox, 1987.

Hoard, Walter B., ed. *Outstanding Black Sermons*. Vol. 2. Valley Forge, Pa.: Judson, 1979.

Johnson, Suzan D., ed. *Wise Women Bearing Gifts: Joys and Struggles of Their Faith*. Valley Forge, Pa.: Judson, 1985.

Lawless, Elaine J. *Handmaidens of the Lord: Pentecostal Women Preachers and Traditional Religion*. Philadelphia: University of Pennsylvania Press, 1988.

Lee, Jarena. "A Female Preacher Among the African Methodists." In *Afro-American Religious History: A Documentary Witness*, edited by Milton C. Sernett, 160–79. Durham, N.C.: Duke University Press, 1985.

Lawrence-Lightfoot, Sarah. *I've Known Rivers: Lives of Loss and Liberation*. Reading, Mass.: Addison-Wesley, 1994.

Lincoln, C. Eric, and Lawrence H. Mamiya. *The Black Church in the African American Experience*. Durham, N.C.: Duke University Press, 1990.

Lischer, Richard. *The Preacher King*. New York: Oxford University Press, 1995.

Mitchell, Timothy. *Colonizing Egypt*. Berkeley: University of California Press, 1991.

Noth, Martin. *The History of Israel*. Translated by Stanley Godman. New York: Harper, 1958.

Official Journal and Year Book of the Delaware Annual Conference 82nd Session, 1944.

Official Journal and Year Book of the Delaware Annual Conference 84th Session, 1946.

Owens, Milton E., Jr., ed. *Outstanding Black Sermons*. Vol. 3. Valley Forge, Pa.: Judson, 1982.

Philpot, William, ed. *Best Black Sermons*. Valley Forge, Pa.: Judson, 1972.

Potter Smith, Sarah. "An Autobiographical Interview Conducted on October 15, 1995." Alison P. Gise-Johnson, interviewer.

Proctor, Samuel D., and William D. Watley. *Sermons from the Black Pulpit*. Valley Forge, Pa.: Judson, 1984.

Raboteau, Albert J. *Slave Religion: The Invisible Institution in Antebellum South*. New York: Oxford University Press, 1978.

———. Foreword by Gardner C. Taylor. *The Certain Sound of the Trumpet: Crafting a Sermon of Authority*. Valley Forge, Pa.: Judson, 1994.

Songs of Zion. Nashville: Abingdon, 1981.

Spearing Randolph, Florence. "The Friends of Wickedness." From the Florence Spearing Randolph Sermon Collection. Philadelphia: Center for African American History and Culture, Temple University.

———. "A Willingness to Help." From the Florence Spearing Randolph Sermon Collection. Philadelphia: Center for African American History and Culture, Temple University.

———. "Woman, the Builder of Her House." From the Florence Spearing Randolph Sermon Collection. Philadelphia: Center for African American History and Culture, Temple University.

Terborg-Penn, Rosalynn. "Historical Treatment of Afro-Americans in the Woman's Movements, 1900–1920: A Biographical Essay." In *Black Women in United States History*, edited by Darlene Clark Hine, 245–59. New York: Carlson Publishing, 1990.

Smith, Alfred J., Sr., ed. *Outstanding Black Sermons*. Valley Forge, Pa.: Judson, 1976.

Walker, Alice. *In Search of Our Mothers' Gardens: Womanist Prose*. San Diego: Harcourt Brace & Company, 1983.

Williams, Delores. "A Womanist Perspective on Sin." In *A Troubling in My Soul: Womanist Perspectives on Evil and Suffering*, edited by Emilie M. Townes, 130–44. Maryknoll, N.Y.: Orbis, 1993.

NOTES

1. Delores Williams defines the invisibilization as the process that makes invisible the womanist character of black women's experience and emphasizes the stereotypical images of black women that prevail and are perpetuated in the larger society. This definition is presented in Delores Williams, "A Womanist Perspective on Sin," in *A Troubling in My Soul: Womanist Perspectives on Evil and Suffering,* ed. Emilie M. Townes (Maryknoll, N.Y.: Orbis, 1993), 146.

2. In *Colonizing Egypt* the term *exhibition* is used to depict European efforts to objectify the culture and history of colonized peoples.

3. Katie Geneva Cannon has begun this process by using literature by and about black women as a source from which to extract the experiences and historical developments of black women and the black community. Specifically she uses the writings of Zora Neale Hurston as the source for her research and analysis in black womanist ethics (Atlanta: Scholars Press, 1988).

4. The interview is one that I conducted with the Reverend Sarah Potter Smith on October 5, 1995, in Philadelphia, Pennsylvania.

5. See Helen Gray Crotwell, *Women and the Word: Sermons* (Philadelphia: Fortress, 1977); Suzan D. Johnson, ed., *Wise Women Bearing Gifts: Joys and Struggles of Their Faith*, vols. 1, 2, and 3 (Valley Forge, Pa.: Judson, 1985); Jarena Lee, "A Female Preacher Among the African Methodists," in *Afro-American Religious History: A Documentary Witness,* ed. Milton C. Sernett (Durham, N.C.: Duke University Press, 1985), 160–79; Ella Pearson Mitchell, ed., *Women: To Preach or Not to Preach: Twenty-One Outstanding Black Preachers Say Yes!* (Valley Forge, Pa.: Judson Press, 1991); Gloria Davis Goode, *Preachers of the Word and Singers of the Gospel: The Ministry of Women Among Nineteenth-Century African Americans* (Philadelphia: University of Pennsylvania Press, 1990); Elaine J. Lawless, *Handmaidens of the Lord: Pentecostal Women Preachers and Traditional Religion* (Philadelphia: University of Pennsylvania Press, 1988); Lewis V. Baldwin, "Black Women and African Union Methodism, 1813–1983," *Methodist History* 21 (1982–1983):225–37; Jualynne Dodson, "Nineteenth-Century A.M.E. Preaching Women: Cutting Edge of Women's Inclusion in Church Polity," in *Women in New Worlds: Historical Perspectives on the Wesleyan Tradition,* ed. Hilah F. Thomas and Rosemary Skinner Keller, 2 vols. (Nashville: Abingdon, 1981–1982), 1:276–89.

6. See Michael A. Battle, ed., *Voices of Experience: Twentieth-Century Prophets Speak* (New York: Martin Luther King Fellows Press, 1985); Charles Emerson Boddie, *God's "Bad Boys"* (Valley Forge, Pa.: Judson, 1985); Walter B. Hoard, ed., *Outstanding Black Sermons*, vol. 2 (Valley Forge, Pa.: Judson, 1979); Milton E. Owens Jr., ed., *Outstanding Black Sermons*, vol. 3 (Valley Forge, Pa.: Judson, 1982); William Philpot, ed., *Best Black Sermons* (Valley Forge: Judson, 1972); Samuel D. Proctor and William D. Watley, *Sermons from the Black Pulpit* (Valley Forge, Pa.: Judson, 1984); Alfred J. Smith Sr., ed., *Outstanding Black Sermons* (Valley Forge, Pa.: Judson, 1976).

7. Such use of the sermon for this purpose may be seen in the contemporary sense in the analysis of the sermons of Dr. Martin Luther King Jr. Recently Richard Lischer has performed this type of analysis in *The Preacher King* (New York: Oxford University Press, 1995).

8. Katie Geneva Cannon, "Womanist Interpretations and Preaching in the Black Church," in *Searching the Scriptures*, ed. Elisabeth Schüssler Fiorenza (New York: Crossroad, 1993), 331.

9. The specifics of how this is accomplished will be discussed in the section outlining the method of analysis to be used in this study.

10. This type of analysis is represented in traditional, liberationist, and womanist approaches to scholarship, which use biblical text as primary source. For traditional representations see John Bright, *A History of Israel*, 2d ed. (Philadelphia: Westminster, 1972); Martin Noth, *The History of Israel*, trans. Stanley Godman (New York: Harper, 1958). In addition, Norman K. Gottwald, *The Hebrew Bible: A Socio-Literary Introduction* (Philadelphia: Fortress, 1985) though considered to be a traditional scholar, develops hypothesis of the history and uses the sermons and other genre present in the text to note socioeconomic developments. Liberationist and womanist scholars use both the New Testament and Old Testament text to consider not only the traditional questions of their disciplines but also the recovery of the presence and theology of women and Africans in the biblical world. See Jacqueline Grant, *White Women's Christ and Black Women's Jesus: Feminist Christology and Womanist Response* (Atlanta: Scholars Press, 1989); Randall C. Bailey, *David in Love and War: The Pursuit of Power in 2 Samuel 10–12* (Sheffield: JSOT Press, 1990); Charles Copher, *Black Biblical Studies: An Anthology of Charles Copher Biblical and Theological Issues on the Black Presence in the Bible* (Chicago: Black Light Fellowship, 1993); Randall C. Bailey and Jacquelyn Grant, eds., *The Recovery of Black Presence: An Interdisciplinary Exploration* (Nashville: Abingdon, 1995); Cain Hope Felder, ed., *Stony the Road We Trod: African American Biblical Interpretation* (Minneapolis: Fortress, 1991).

11. See Rosalynn Terborg-Penn, "Historical Treatment of Afro-Americans in the Woman's Movements, 1900–1920: A Biographical Essay," in *Black Women in United States History*, ed. Darlene Clark Hine (New York: Carlson Publishing, 1990), 245–59.

12. Katie Geneva Cannon, "Hitting a Straight Lick with a Crooked Stick: The Womanist Dilemma in the Development of a Black Liberation Ethic," in *Feminist Theological Ethics*, ed. Lois K. Daly (Louisville, Ky.: Westminster/John Knox), 35.

13. John Hayes and Carl R. Holladay, *Biblical Exegesis: A Beginner's Handbook* (Atlanta: John Knox, 1987), 24.

14. Ibid., 26–29. Following are the definitions of each type of criticism: textual criticism reestablishes the original wording or reading of the text; historical establishes the setting in time or the historical, geographical, and cultural setting or the context of the original author(s) and audience(s) by taking note of certain customs, events, places, and names referred to in the text; grammatical criticism includes attempts to answer questions pertaining to the language of the text; literary is concerned with the style, character, composition techniques, and rhetorical patterns; form is concerned with the passage or with subunits in a passage, and special attention is given to the literary form or genre of the passage; tradition is employed in efforts to uncover the earlier stages of development through which a text has passed, an approach that is appropriate in the analysis of sermons that have been preached more than once or the discovery and analysis of drafts of the text; redaction focuses on the final form of the passage and the changes or redaction it may have undergone in the editorial process; structural seeks to explain how the meaning is structured into a text, to understand how a reader comprehends a text, and to discover how universal structures of thought open the text to the reader. Thus the text is read without regard to its origins, the author's intention, and the original audience.

15. Human archaeology is a critical method of inquiry developed and being developed by Dr. Sarah Lawrence-Lightfoot. It was first articulated in *I've Known Rivers: Lives of Loss and Liberation* (Reading, Mass.: Addison-Wesley, 1994). Currently she is writing a book to articulate this critical method more in depth.

16. Cannon, "Hitting a Straight Lick with a Crooked Stick," 37.

17. Cannon, "Womanist Interpretation and Preaching in the Black Church," 326–37.

18. "His Eye Is on the Sparrow" is the name of a hymn written by Civilla D. Martin (1860–1948) and Charles H. Gabriel (1856–1932). This song is published in many hymnals. The dates of the composers reflected here were found in *Songs of Zion* (Nashville: Abingdon, 1981), the songbook for black United Methodist worship.

19. *Official Journal and Year Book of the Delaware Annual Conference 84th Session*, 1946, 346.

20. *Official Journal and Year Book of the Delaware Annual Conference 82nd Session*, 1944, 125.

21. In the Methodist tradition even to the present, the denomination publishes what is called *The Book of Discipline*. This text outlines the rights and duties of each organization existing in the local church, the responsibilities of the members as Christian Methodists, the theological posture, and the rights and duties of the pastors who serve in local churches and other positions constructed and controlled by the denomination.

22. The terms *anthropology, pneumatology,* and *theology* in traditional theological usage describe the discourse of the nature of humankind, the Holy Spirit, and God, respectively.

23. The Hegelian methodology refers to the dialectic found in the writings

of George Wilhelm Friedrich Hegel (1770–1831). This dialectical approach was designed to search for truth.

24. Samuel D. Proctor, Foreword by Gardner C. Taylor, *The Certain Sound of the Trumpet: Crafting a Sermon of Authority* (Valley Forge, Pa.: Judson, 1994), 28.

25. The Reverend Florence Spearing Randolph, "The Friends of Wickedness," from the Florence Spearing Randolph Sermon Collection (Philadelphia: Center for African American History and Culture, Temple University). This pattern is also noted in "Woman, the Builder of Her House" and "A Willingness to Help."

26. Cannon, "Womanist Interpretations and Preaching in the Black Church," 326, 327.

27. See Albert J. Raboteau, *Slave Religion: The Invisible Institution in Antebellum South* (New York: Oxford University Press, 1978).

28. Evidenced in the following sermons: "Hope," "The Friends of Wickedness," "Woman, the Builder of Her House," and "A Willingness to Help."

29. See the sermon "Hope."

30. Ibid.

31. This terminology of self-abnegation and self-forgetfulness appear in two texts. They are observed in "Hope" and "A Willingness to Help." This is of interest because these sermons were preached in 1909 and 1946, respectively.

32. Jacqueline Grant, "Black Theology and the Black Woman," in *Black Theology: A Documentary History,* vol. 1, *1966–1979,* ed. James Cone and Gayraud S. Wilmore (Maryknoll, N.Y.: Orbis, 1993), 331, 332.

CHAPTER 10

A WORTHY LEGACY
Preaching to Teach

GLORIA C. TAYLOR

Since the organization of the black church in the last half of the eighteenth century, the sermon has held a place of unequaled importance. At that time black preachers accomplished several objectives through the sermon. Of course the major purpose of the sermon was to win converts to the Christian faith and to offer the promise of a better life in the hereafter. In addition, however, the sermon was the primary means by which newly freed blacks received the education that was considered a necessity for being a Christian as well as for survival in this country. This trend of preaching and teaching continued well into the next hundred years. The black church grew phenomenally, becoming the institution of dominance in black culture. With this growth, it became — and has remained — very preaching-oriented. This fact may be related to what has been reported by Colleen Birchett in *A History of Religious Education in the Black Church*. Birchett reports that during the latter half of the nineteenth century, there were vigorous religious education programs for blacks through churches and missionary societies. But as the church moved into the twentieth century it faced the problem of uneducated clergy.[1] With fewer than 5 percent of clergy having any training at all, their participation in the education of persons in the pew became almost nonexistent. It has only been during the latter half of the twentieth century that churches have given renewed attention to Christian education as a vital and distinct ministry component. This chapter will examine how much of the teaching done in and by the church evolved from the basic method of teaching via the Sunday sermon. Several suggestions will then be made in support of the important and fundamental role of the pastor as teacher, both formally and informally. Finally, clues will be provided to show reason for pastors to take ever more seriously their role as teacher-in-residence using sermons as one method. The focus will be on sermons that are by intent and design teaching sermons. This will be done with an eye on the challenges facing Christians and the church in the twenty-first century.

FROM PREACHING AND TEACHING TO PREACHING

The latter half of the twentieth century has been a time of increase in the development of intentional, structured, and holistic programs of Christian education. Pastors have accepted that a fundamental role and responsibility of pastoral leadership is to educate Christians in all aspects of daily life. Teaching in the black church may be attributed in large measure to the legacy of what Henry H. Mitchell calls "the Black Fathers" — those black pastors serving in churches that were primarily under black control, from the late eighteenth century to the early twentieth century.[2] In most cases the Black Fathers were the only persons who had acquired any formal education; thus they became both preacher and teacher. Mitchell reminds us that these men made strenuous efforts to establish schools and train others coming on behind them. Teaching others was no small feat considering that their education had in all probability been acquired under extreme adversity and many of them were largely self-educated.

By the middle of this twentieth century, a renewed focus on cultural heritage studies had served as a stern reminder of the emphasis on education that was a persistent part of life for the newly freed blacks of the late eighteenth and early nineteenth century. Mitchell also calls attention to the fact that the twentieth-century church has been blessed by numbers of black master preachers who were nurtured in the tradition of the Black Fathers and polished by the black colleges and seminaries founded by the churches.[3]

The Black Fathers were not only good teachers and powerful preachers; they were also talented organizers who put their skills to work in the black community, working against insurmountable odds. In teaching, the Black Fathers exhibited more vision and foresight than they received credit for. They focused on needs-based education and sought to provide knowledge and skills that would be useful for the simple tasks of living daily. These Fathers were unaware of all that we now know about the importance of meeting needs or about stages of human growth and development. There was neither time nor inclination to reflect on an idea such as learner readiness. Hence, while lacking in the tools of psychology, sociology, economics, political science, or even a systematized theology, black preachers were among the first blacks to seek first to improve themselves through schooling and then to educate others. Of course much of the teaching had to be done clandestinely since blacks were still forbidden to congregate in separate groupings, but the slaves were as persistent in their desire to be educated as the Fathers were to teach them. Education was tied to their religion, and literacy was thought to be the key to the Scriptures, the Word of God. The Black Fathers considered education an absolute necessity especially for the men who would preach, teach, and otherwise lead God's people.

By the late nineteenth century, many of the black preachers had advanced to the status of professional teachers in the public schools and academies. In most cases these men were well received and respected and were responsible for the uplift of their race through learning. One identifying characteristic of the early preachers was that they did not function from a leadership hierarchy. They considered themselves one of the people; they knew what the basic needs of the people were and sought to meet those needs in the best way possible under the circumstances. As interpreters of the Bible, the preachers focused on communicating truth that would comfort, strengthen, and guide the freed slaves. Their educational goal was twofold: to equip black people to survive in a hostile white world and — strengthened by their faith in Jesus Christ — to keep alive their African cultural heritage.

The sermon was practically the only medium for communicating truth, and it was skillfully and creatively used to uplift the black race. It was crafted as a highly imaginative approach to the gospel, and the preacher sought to make it relevant to black culture and situation. The sermon was organized for the total good of people — politically, economically, and educationally. Always in preaching there was evident an active concern for black freedom.[4] Because of its prominence as the Word of God, delivered through a human vessel, lay Christians may have been led to believe that the sermon was the only form of education available through the church. As time moved on and access to higher education became possible for more laypersons fewer pastors were found in the classroom. This change may have led laity to believe that the sole function of pastors was to preach. The matter of pastoral preaching and teaching has undergone several changes. Nevertheless, preaching and teaching have remained major foci of African American church ministry. Traditionally both have been promoted from the pulpit with emphasis on the Bible and education for Christian living.

Sermons in the black tradition have served to advance Christian growth and maturity, to promote healing and wholeness, and to build a healthy self-esteem among a people who have known — and still experience — a spiritual deficit called low self-esteem.[5] Mitchell and his coauthor Emil Thomas have reminded us that "a sound definition of self-esteem that is rooted in the Holy Scriptures can only enhance the traditional role of the Black church as a guarantor of the survival of Black people in America."[6] The authors characterize the book as a laser-like focus on preaching as a ministry to enhance the ethnic self-esteem of African Americans.[7] This also follows and is consistent with the precedent set by the Black Fathers, who obviously had the whole person in mind as they preached to and also taught the people, preparing them for life in their present reality and in God's eternal kingdom.

THE PASTOR AS TEACHER

In the tradition of the Black Fathers, pastoral leaders must continue to adhere to the dual mandate to preach and teach. Clearly Ephesians 4:11 provides scriptural basis for this responsibility and establishes it as the most important role of a pastor. To fulfill this role, Robert Pazmiño says the church has been provided with an agenda for its education ministry. The agenda — made explicit in Matthew 28:18–20 — includes a challenge to the church: nurture and teach all that Jesus taught.[8] Education as a distinct ministry of the church is a scriptural mandate. Authors of a recent curriculum guide agree and suggest and explain five inescapable reasons why the church must educate: Christ expects it; the gospel demands it; history proves it; people need it; and the current situation requires it.[9] Even without benefit of the explanation, these five reasons deserve serious reflection and demand careful attention for both preaching and teaching as the church moves further into the twenty-first century. The five reasons form the basis for worship preparation as well as curriculum resource selection. Curriculum in relation to these five reasons is understood to refer to all the facets of the church's life and to include all the relationships and experiences shared by persons in the gathered community, including the experience of worship. This form of curriculum design calls for more deliberate and intentional planning of education.

Among today's churchgoers are large numbers of persons who have little or no foundation in biblical knowledge but who are seeking and searching for answers to life's perennial questions: Who am I? What is my purpose in life? How can I live in the world today in a more Christ-like manner? How do I come to truly know God? With the decline in attendance at the traditional Sunday church school, which most churches have experienced, the worship experience may again (as in earlier days) be the only time for serious learning for most and the best time for learning for many. Therefore the sermon takes on even greater significance. Real learning results in change in four growth areas: cognitive/thinking, affective/feeling, volitional/deciding, and behavioral/doing. As mentioned earlier, Christian education attends to the whole person and thus addresses each growth area. The corporate worship experience combines all these areas in what has always been the central and binding experience of the community of faith. Israel Galindo includes a chapter on "Worship as Christian Education" in a recent book on Christian teaching.[10] He offers the chapter as an invitation to widen our definition of Christian education. Galindo, opting for more attention to the worship experience while not minimizing the impact of Sunday school, says when worship is done well, it is the most significant education event in the average church week. Worship is central because "in essence it is the confession that 'God is God, and we are God's people.'"[11] Worship, or the preparation for it, is the domain of the pastor; thus the responsibility for what will happen to the participant is likewise his or hers. Specifically the impact of the sermon is the preacher's burden to teach as well as to inspire.

Mitchell believes the sermon must have an intentional educational focus. Responding to an interview question on sermon purpose, he replied that the sermon ought to have a behavioral objective, that is, it should result in some change in the hearer's knowing, feeling, or doing. It is noteworthy that Mitchell used educational terms in his response. When preparing a lesson, the teacher usually thinks of learning objectives; what would be the desirable effect on the learner, that is, what would the learner be able to be or do as result of participation in the teaching/learning experience. The same question can be applied to sermon preparation. Although the purpose of the sermon is never exclusively to educate, it should contain an educational component. Something should happen to the hearer of the sermon that would result at bare minimum in consideration of a lifestyle change, a transformation. The impact of the sermon can be enhanced significantly when it is developed according to educational guidelines and principles. As Mitchell says in amplifying his interview answer, the "main result of the sermon has to be in the hearer."[12] This result is predetermined by the sermon goal and objective.

By the dawn of the twentieth century there had been a significant increase in number of black churches, but there were a limited number of schools, in particular seminaries, that would accept blacks for higher education. The situation was that churches needed preachers. Hence the church issued a call and someone who had acknowledged a call to preach responded. Consequently many black churches had pastors with little or no theological education.

Following in the tradition of the Black Fathers, preachers continued to be concerned about the uplift of black brothers and sisters, and so took other steps to become educated and trained for ministry. After the civil rights movement, which included the social revolution of the 1970s, black pastors became much more concerned about their ability to lead people with honesty and integrity. Where necessary they sought help and advice about how best to acquire theological training for themselves and to be able to provide more opportunities for the education of laity within their charge. One example is the program of continuing education at the Samuel DeWitt Proctor School of Theology at Virginia Union University in Richmond, Virginia. The program started in the 1970s with a few black pastors — some with limited formal education in the liberal arts, but none with theological education — requesting assistance from the seminary faculty. They desired to become biblically and theologically literate while also gaining administrative and organizational skills to be more effective pastors. Not only did these pastors desire education for themselves; they also expressed a need to be able to teach their people.

During the tenure of Henry Mitchell as dean of the STVU and Ella Mitchell as director of continuing education, the program was revised to give a more comprehensive focus to the education being provided for such pastors. The revision included the addition of new courses, new course descriptions, and a name change from Education for Leadership in the Black Church to the Evans-Smith Leadership Training Institute.[13] The ELT Institute, now in its twenty-fifth year, continues to satisfy a need for many who lack educational prerequisites for seminary matriculation but who nevertheless desire to fulfill the call of God to minister in a pastoral role, successfully preaching and teaching.

In the 1990 study that profiled the black church and black religion, authors C. Eric Lincoln and Lawrence H. Mamiya reported that "no other area of black life received a higher priority from black churches than education."[14] Not unlike their slave ancestors, African American Christians still believe education is the means to a better quality of life. Christians in most churches still appreciate, indeed look forward with anticipation to, the pastor's teaching. This is most true in cases where the pastor is seminary trained, leads with a vision, and feels a sense of compulsion and urgency to teach the congregation.

Following is an excerpt from an article about the dynamic teaching of one pastor who led the church to adopt an alternative church school program in response to the need to provide educational experiences for all persons, particularly adults. This program was begun in the aftermath of the civil rights movement and has had great success as a teaching ministry. As author Sid Smith writes about the holistic approach to ministry at this church (New Shiloh Baptist, Baltimore, Maryland) he includes a conscientious concern for the education of the whole person, stressing the important and dynamic teaching role of the church's pastor, Dr. Harold A. Carter.

> One cannot help but be impressed with the skills of the pastor in the area of teaching. The full weight of his theological training enriches the class taught by the pastor on Saturday mornings. . . . One senses that the audience does not hesitate to ask difficult questions because their teacher probably knows the answer.[15]

The alternative church school program at New Shiloh is one example among many where the pastor has demonstrated keen awareness of the educational needs of the people. Smith also calls attention to the fact that this pastor is a giant in the pulpit, a great orator, and a great journalist. However, it was this pastor's vision, creativity, and determination to move education to center stage that caused him to give the leadership needed to help the church become a true teaching church.

TEACHING VIA SERMONS

The church has always witnessed to the importance of teaching, although at times it has seemed to minimize some aspects of the teaching ministry. One such aspect has been the sermon as a basic teaching occasion. The current situation (referred to above as the fifth inescapable reason for Christian education) demands a recovery of this essential understanding of pastoral ministry. Although the pastor's role has changed much and is still undergoing renewal, teaching as fundamental has not been obscured. The time is ripe for pastors to utilize more teaching sermons. Ronald J. Allen identifies the teaching sermon not so much by its form or method but by its purpose. "The primary purpose of a teaching sermon is to help the congregation name (or rename) some aspect of its world experience in terms of the gospel. The sermon is consciously designed to encourage the community to grow in some aspect of Christian awareness or action."[16] Pastors today may have several assistants and associates who assist with the teaching. Competent laypersons are assuming many duties previously performed by the pastor. However, there are many church members who still consider the pastor as the main educational resource person. Also, not to be ignored are those very small churches where the pastor functions much like the Black Fathers of old — teaching, preaching, and helping with life skills. Indeed the modern pastor as teacher still has the rare privilege of being available to God's people as a resource, in whatever ways their lives may require assistance. To teach or not to teach is not the question; the issue may be how much and what kind of teaching the pastor will do. After suggesting that pastors decide how much time and energy they would be willing to devote to the important teaching ministry, David Evans reflected that perhaps a more significant question for pastors is this: Are we ever not involved in the church's teaching ministry?[17] The answer is probably a resounding no, at least for the pastor who has the welfare of the people at heart and is concerned about the totality of human beings.

Writing on the subject of "What the Pastor Teaches" Samuel Proctor identified seven areas where the pastor must be prepared as teacher: how to apply the gospel to personal behavior, to civic orientation, to political choices, to stewardship, to health care and management, to intercultural relations, to one's view of the world. This is not to be considered an exhaustive list. Proctor added that there are others and even important subsets of these. Pastors, because they are near, informed, and accessible, must also deal with the more practical and mundane aspects of life.[18] Teaching responsibilities run the gamut. The witness of the early church needs explanation. The pastor is perceived to be the teacher of lay teachers. He or she must share with new members in the faith that the mission of the church is symbolized in its various ministries of *kerygma, liturgia, koinonia, diakonia,* and *didache.* Senior adults need assistance as they prepare for retirement and apply for Social Security, and again the pastor may be the only person knowledgeable enough to initiate the process. There is great need to discuss with youth why "just say no" may not be sufficient. In the faith community where all persons are in a state of growth and change, opportunities to teach surface constantly. One of the pastor's main teaching responsibilities is to teach the volunteer lay church teachers. These volunteers are given the task of forming others in the faith, yet as pointed out by James Evans, most churches put little emphasis on the educational ministry. He says:

> Many churches will spare no expense to ensure that they obtain a leader who is skilled in preaching and fund-raising, but rely on volunteers who have received very little training to run their Christian education programs.[19]

Even when the pastor does not teach personally, he or she is expected to be responsible to see that teaching happens and that it is effective.

People speak of a new paradigm for the church but are often unprepared to say what that is. It may be that a recovery of teaching and learning is what is most needed as the church moves further into the twenty-first century. The pastor is a primary figure in this recovery; making careful, intentional, and prayerful use of the method always at his or her disposal — the sermon. This is a perfect opportunity to invite people to grow in faith. Faith growth has become the raison d'être of the church's ministry of Christian education since Thomas Groome's landmark work of 1980, in which he established the purpose of Christian education as being to enable persons to live as Christians, that is, to live lives of Christian faith.[20] The church must use every means possible to ensure that all persons receive equal opportunity to study and grow in faith. The sermon can be a genuine help to a congregation's faith learning. The sermon can be a true teaching moment, providing tremendous help in increasing the faith maturity level of parishioners.

The church must take seriously the lack of adequate teaching of the faith. It must remember that ministry is never reducible to one function, whether it be proclamation, working for justice, or evangelism. Yet none of these functions can ever adequately be done apart from teaching the meaning of the faith. It is dangerous to assume that persons understand the functions just because they have been in the church for years. Likewise, biblical literacy cannot be assumed, even for those who teach regularly. The church is like a system in which each part affects and is affected by every other part. Teaching the meaning of the Christian faith may be the one key to understanding all the other ministerial functions. This will reinforce preaching and evangelism and foster the creation of caring congregations. The onus is on the pastor with seminary training.

As mentioned earlier, the main purpose of the sermon is not to teach, although all sermons have teaching dimensions and indeed do teach, explicitly and implicitly. The preacher who obviously does not spend sufficient time developing the sermon text may implicitly be teaching congregants that it is not necessary to spend long periods of time examining the Scriptures in an attempt to ascertain what God is saying to them as Christians and how God's Word relates to their daily lives.

According to Allen the teaching sermon serves a variety of purposes. One may provide information and argument. Another may create an effective experience (with critical reflection). Still another may analyze some behavior of the congregation or the world. Allen suggests when preaching in a teaching mode, the pastor

> assists the congregation to have a clear view of the subject;
> sets out the importance of the subject to the Christian community;
> helps the community in critical reflection on the topic;
> places the subject in relationship with the congregation's larger worlds;
> encourages the congregation to see how Christian teaching relates to their
>   daily thought, feeling, and practice.[21]

Preaching in the twenty-first century will need to be authoritative messages from God. Persons come to church to hear what God has to say through the pastor/teacher. The pastor's preparation will include research, questions, answers, and a fundamental understanding of the teaching of the text and issues related to the text. There should be a mixture of theory and practical application. Persons want to know how the Bible's truths and principles can be translated into transformed lives. Important considerations for the pastor include discerning what the congregation needs to know and deciding how to correlate that need with the resources in the Bible. The pastor should know the congregation, and the sermon should be customized to fit that audience. The gospel should be declared in a conversation style rather than a lecture, and it must be made to speak to contemporary persons and their needs. The sermon is an experiential encounter with human life transformation as its aim. Sermon development requires holistic goals and methods that affect all sectors of human consciousness. Henry Mitchell believes this is most important if the efforts of the pastor/preacher are to be used by the Holy Spirit to plant faith in the deepest and most complete sense. Every sermon, he says, must make sense and be generally consistent with an orderly understanding of God's creation and our experience in it.[22] Sermon integrity is vital. This means that effective preaching for the twenty-first century will be based on the Word of God first and all other concerns and issues second.

The sermon is a vital teaching tool, and without it the Christian education ministry of churches will be inadequate to lead persons to God in Christ. There is an urgent need to recover this authentic Christian teaching approach that has a long history in the life of the church. Henry Mitchell has reminded the black church that we have a legacy that should not be forgotten. In that tradition, he says:

> Indeed the struggles of the Black Fathers should obligate their sons (and daughters) in the ministry — wherever they are trained — to sort out whatever is good, whatever is viable for Black interests, whatever can be refined and translated for the cause. If religion in America is going to survive at all, it may well be that its survival depends on what Black Christians do about it.[23]

NOTES

1. Colleen Birchett, "A History of Religious Education in the Black Church," in *Urban Church Education*, ed. Donald B. Rogers (Birmingham, Ala.: Religious Education Press, 1989), 74–76.

2. Henry H. Mitchell, *Black Preaching* (New York: Harper & Row, 1979), 52.

3. Ibid., 52–58.

4. Ibid., 47.

5. Henry H. Mitchell and Emil M. Thomas, *Preaching for Black Self-Esteem* (Nashville: Abingdon, 1994), 10.

6. Ibid., 26.

7. Ibid., 153.

8. Robert W. Pazmiño, *Foundational Issues in Christian Education* (Grand Rapids, Mich.: Baker, 1988), 29–30.

9. Howard P. Colson and Raymond M. Rigdon, *Understanding Your Church's Curriculum* (Nashville: Broadman, 1981), 15–20.

10. Israel Galindo, *The Craft of Christian Teaching* (Valley Forge, Pa.: Judson, 1998), 61–67.

11. Ibid.

12. Kirk Byron Jones, "An Interview with Henry H. Mitchell," in *The African American Pulpit* 1, no. 1 (winter 1997–88): 88.

13. The new name honors two black parents who espoused the cause of education as a means of being faithful to God and as a means of freedom: Dr. Charles L. Evans, former executive secretary for the Baptist General Convention of Virginia and Mrs. Lena M. Smith, former director of Christian education and women's work for the state convention (BGC).

14. C. Eric Lincoln and Lawrence H. Mamiya, *The Black Church in the African American Experience* (Durham, N.C.: Duke University Press, 1990), 251.

15. Gayraud S. Wilmore, ed., *African American Religious Studies: An Interdisciplinary Anthology* (Durham, N.C.: Duke University Press, 1992), 410.

16. Ronald J. Allen, *The Teaching Sermon* (Nashville: Abingdon, 1995), 36.

17. David M. Evans, *The Pastor in a Teaching Church* (Valley Forge, Pa.: Judson, 1983), 12.

18. Samuel D. Proctor and Gardner C. Taylor, *We Have This Ministry: The Heart of the Pastor's Vocation* (Valley Forge, Pa.: Judson, 1996), 16–17.

19. James H. Evans Jr., *We Have Been Believers* (Minneapolis: Fortress, 1992), 170–71, n. 60.

20. Thomas H. Groome, *Christian Religious Education* (San Francisco: Harper & Row, 1980), 34.

21. Allen, 37.

22. Henry H. Mitchell, *Celebration and Experience in Preaching* (Nashville: Abingdon, 1990), 18, 21.

23. Mitchell, *Black Preaching,* 63–64.

ABOUT THE CONTRIBUTORS

All of the contributors noted here are members of the faculty of the Samuel DeWitt Proctor School of Theology of Virginia Union University, Richmond, Virginia.

NATHAN DELL, M.DIV., is instructor of homiletics. He served as pastor of the Woodville Presbyterian Church in Richmond for thirty-two years (1964–1996).

PATRICIA A. GOULD-CHAMP, ED.D., is assistant professor of practical theology. She is also the senior pastor of Faith Community Baptist Church in Richmond.

ALISON P. GISE JOHNSON, Ph.D. candidate, is assistant professor of theology and ethics. Her research and teaching interests are in the area of African American womanist hermeneutics.

MILES JEROME JONES, M.A., is professor of homiletics. He has served for thirty-five years as pastor of congregations in the Richmond area.

VICTORIA L. PRATT, M.DIV., is instructor of practical theology. Her interests lie in spirituality and the interplay between religion and wholeness.

SAMUEL KELTON ROBERTS, PH.D., is professor of Christian ethics. His research and writing interests lie in theological and virtue ethics.

JEROME CLAYTON ROSS, PH.D., is assistant professor of Old Testament and Hebrew. His research interests lie in biblical law and Israelite history and culture.

BOYKIN SANDERS, PH.D., is professor of New Testament and Greek. His research interests lie in the areas of the biblical canon and Pauline writings.

GLORIA C. TAYLOR, ED.D., is assistant professor of Christian education. Dr. Taylor is currently working on a program to expand and enrich local congregational ministries of Christian education.

ROBERT WAFAWANAKA, TH.D., is assistant professor of biblical studies and Old Testament. His research and teaching interests are in Israelite literature, biblical Hebrew, and poverty and wealth in the Bible.